R K Bürgen

Feb. 18, 2016

COURAGEOUS
DISSENT

Hiram Bingham IV, circa 1980.

How Harry Bingham
        Defied His Government
    To Save Lives

COURAGEOUS DISSENT

Robert Kim Bingham, Sr.

Courageous Dissent: How Harry Bingham Defied
His Government to Save Lives
by Robert Kim Bingham, Sr.

First Edition, 2007
Second Edition, 2009

ISBN: 0-9613602-3-2
ISBN-13: 978-0-9613602-3-8

Contact Robert K. Bingham
Salem, Connecticut
Email rbingham03@snet.net

Design: Nina Miller Design
Cover design: Linda Wade

Printed in the United States of America

This book is dedicated to Rose and Harry Bingham,
loving parents of eleven children.

Hiram Bingham certainly personifies the kind of leadership and courage that we like to think that we instill in our students. . . .

Bingham is a true hero who rose to a dangerous occasion, thought for himself, and did what was right.

—Richard Levin
President of Yale University

Contents

Preface

The Harry Bingham I knew for forty-five years, who was born in Cambridge, Massachusetts, on July 17, 1903, was a generous upbeat man, full of ideas and compassion. Tall and slender, he had a shock of white hair and round gold wire-rimmed glasses that magnified his brown eyes, making him look like a sage old owl. I remember a man who was always looking for the best in people. Seeing a silver lining in every situation freed him from discouragement over setbacks.

My father and I had many lively talks around the dining-room table of our family home in Salem, Connecticut, about government and politics. He and his father and two of his brothers had all worked in government, and I followed in their footsteps. When I started my career as a U.S. Justice Department lawyer in 1972, my father urged me to exercise compassion in my job and not administer authority harshly.

This advice took on new significance years later when I learned more about his own actions in Marseilles, France. We would talk about right and wrong, and the need to do right—whatever the cost. I learned many lessons from him; but it was only after his death that I learned the greatest lesson, that sometimes to do right, to stand up to evil, you have to defy the system—and be prepared to suffer the consequences.

And what was it that Harry Bingham did, that he suppressed for most of his life, and that only recently has publicly spotlighted my father as the hero I always knew him to be? It is my purpose to disclose in the following pages some details of this quiet hero's actions and to reveal the tribute to his memory I have labored to achieve.

Hiram ("Harry") Bingham IV was the second of seven sons of explorer Hiram Bingham III, who discovered Machu Picchu in Peru in 1911, and Alfreda Mitchell Bingham Gregor, granddaughter of Tiffany and Company founder, Charles Tiffany. Harry died in Salem, Connecticut, where he lived for the last forty-two years of his life, on January 12, 1988, at age eighty-four.

He was educated at Groton School and Yale University, and attended Harvard Law School until he achieved a high score on a U.S. Foreign Service entrance examination and began his career with the Foreign Service in the Far East.

From 1937 to 1941, the State Department assigned him to the post of U.S. vice consul in Marseilles, France. While there, he defied his department's restrictive immigration policies by liberally writing visas for refugees from the Holocaust, sometimes hiding them in his diplomatic residence, and coordinating their escape from France to America and freedom. Harry Bingham helped save renowned Jewish artists, painters, and intellectuals, such as painter Marc Chagall, anti-Nazi author Lion Feuchtwanger, Nobel Prize physicist Otto Meyerhof, and many other less well-known Jewish and non-Jewish refugees. In 1941, he was reassigned to Buenos Aires, Argentina, far away from Europe. There he was denied promotions by the State Department, and he resigned from the Foreign Service in 1945, returning with his wife Rose and their children to bucolic Salem, Connecticut, where he had inherited a farm and five-hundred acres of fields and woodlands. Our house, built in 1769 by ancestor John Mumford, which remained in and out of the family since that time, was the delightful place where I and my ten siblings grew up.

I have asked myself why Harry did not talk to me about his "dissent" from his superiors in the State Department. Maybe he did not want to toot his own horn—he was like that. Perhaps it was too complicated trying to defend breaking the law, even if it was for a greater good; he was a stickler for playing by the rules. Or maybe he was haunted by the lengthy, daily lines of humans he could not save. One time he mentioned the endless lines of refugees outside consulates in Europe, and while muttering that "they were treated like cattle," his face turned ashen, his frowns became pronounced, and he quickly changed the subject. The following pages may shed some light on the silence he kept until his death.

The reasons that he had not discussed his "dissent" prompted me to learn more about that chapter in his life. And as I found out more, I realized here was an astonishing story that should be told.

Sixty-two years after their actions in Marseilles, Harry Bingham and other World War II "righteous and honorable diplomats" from around the world, who had defied their governments' closed-door policies in some of the darkest days of the Holocaust, were finally being recognized for courageously placing humanity above their own careers.

The first inkling I had that he was recognized as a hero by someone outside the family came from invitations sent to Rose and Harry from the U.S. Holocaust Memorial Museum to attend a majestic "Tribute to Rescuers" at the Arlington National

Cemetery in April 1993. My sister Abigail and I did attend the colorful event in place of our parents. Harry had died five years before, and Rose's failing health prevented her from making the trip. I later learned that Varian Fry curators at the U.S. Holocaust Museum had urged Eric Saul in 1996 to include Bingham in his world-traveling "Visas for Life" exhibit, which honored World War II diplomatic rescuers. Two years later, in April 1998, Bingham was featured in the Yad Vashem exhibit in Jerusalem.

When I was a boy, my father and I spent many joyous hours together collecting stamps. Ten years after his death, during a tour of Israel in 1998—at the time of Eric Saul's Yad Vashem exhibit—I met many grateful survivors who were saved by diplomats. I also saw the unveiling of Israeli stamps depicting such diplomats. It was not long before I realized that getting a U.S. postage stamp issued in my father's honor would be the perfect way to spread word of his deeds and to remember those happy times with him. This book also chronicles that adventure—what I learned about Harry from my stamp-drive experience. I am pleased to have contributed to the effort of bringing about a U.S. commemorative stamp in honor of my father.

Robert Kim Bingham, Sr.
Harry Bingham's Sixth of Eleven Children
October 1, 2006

Acknowledgments

This book is, in large measure, an expression of gratitude to the supporters of the successful Hiram Bingham IV stamp campaign, to whom I, as initiator and coordinator of the campaign for six long years, owe a permanent debt of gratitude.

For me, the stamp campaign has been an incredible journey. I consider it a miracle to have found five of Bingham's living survivors over the Internet, who told me their stories about escaping Hitler with Bingham's help and who have enthusiastically participated in the drive: Rabbi Joseph Schachter, Lilian Stuart Smith, Ralph Hockley, Pierre Shostal, and Elly Sherman. Some of them also provided me with copies of their life-saving family visas, signed by Harry Bingham, which I posted on my stamp-drive website (Google my name, Robert Kim Bingham).

Though all those who gave generously of their time in the campaign compose a substantial list, I will first recognize Ilene Munetz Pachman of Pennsylvania, a freelance writer, who—almost from the outset of the campaign in December 1998—has been an inspiration and astute quarterback. A veteran of the successful 1996 Raoul Wallenberg stamp campaign, she continually thought of new strategies and helpful people to contact, and prodded politicians and me to follow things up. She wrote a key *Washington Post* article (July 28, 2001), entitled "Honor This Hero," in which she urged Secretary of State Colin Powell to support the Bingham stamp proposal.

Next, I thank Sherry Hickey of Senator Joseph Lieberman's office for her pivotal cooperation throughout the campaign.

Without her support, I would not even have met Ilene Pachman, nor made vital contacts on Capitol Hill.

I am equally indebted to Connecticut Senators Joseph Lieberman and Christopher Dodd for writing several letters of support to the Citizens' Stamp Advisory Committee and to the U.S. Postmaster General; to Congressman Rob Simmons, for his yeoman efforts; to former Congressman Sam Gejdenson, Governor M. Jodi Rell, former Governor John Rowland; to Susan Bysiewicz, Connnecticut secretary of state; and to Linda Orange, state representative, for writing letters of support; and I thank all 36 Connecticut state senators and 151 state representatives for their amazing unanimous endorsement of the Hiram Bingham IV stamp in 2001. I am grateful to the 40 U.S. Senators and 36 U.S. Representatives who also provided strong bipartisan support for the stamp by signing "Dear Colleague" letters that were forwarded to the U.S. Postal Service.

Particular thanks go to Eric Saul, director of the "Visas for Life" program at the Simon Wiesenthal Center, Los Angeles, who has been a key early supporter of the Hiram Bingham IV stamp since 1999, and whose research and world-traveling "Visas for Life" exhibit continue to shed light on Bingham's role as a part of the ever-expanding group of "righteous and honorable" World War II diplomats; I wish to thank the Simon Wiesenthal Center, Los Angeles, for my family's inspiring tour of Israel in April 1998 for children of "righteous and honorable diplomats," honored during Israel's Fiftieth Anniversary celebrations. We children of the World War II diplomats heard poignant stories of Holocaust survivors who expressed their profound gratitude to the diplomat rescuers. I wish to thank the U.S. Holocaust Memorial Museum.

I am grateful to the American Foreign Service Association and its former president, John K. Naland, and its board of directors for posthumously granting Bingham the "Constructive Dissent" award at a State Department tribute on June 27, 2002; and I thank then Secretary of State Colin Powell for welcoming the Harry Bingham family to this ceremony, publicly praising Bingham in a speech to current and former U.S. diplomats, and personally presenting the American Foreign Service Association's award to his children.

I thank James C. Miller, chairman of the Board of Governors of the U.S. Postal Service, Postmaster General Jack Potter, and Dr. Virginia Noelke, then Chairperson of the Citizens' Stamp Advisory Committee, for their farsighted decision to include Bingham's postage stamp in the series of six "Distinguished American Diplomats," issued on May 30, 2006.

I also extend my thanks to my sister Abigail Endicott and my brothers William and David. I especially thank Abigail's husband, William T. Endicott, for unearthing long-dormant documents and evidentiary material, interviewing survivor Lilian (Winkler) Stuart Smith, and providing persuasive material for the stamp-drive website. I thank William Endicott for his invaluable advice on the manuscript, copious edits, and reworking of chapter 1 to lend a historical context to Harry Bingham's deeds in Marseilles (and Harry's subsequent efforts against the Nazis in Buenos Aires, Argentina), which make the book into more of an educational resource than a mere family memoir. I also thank my cousin, Douglas Bingham, for providing technical service to the stamp-drive website.

I thank Anne Carr Bingham, my dear wife, for her brilliant

observations, inspiration, and editorial assistance; and my brother Hiram ("Tony") Bingham V for his encouragement and tips regarding the design and publication of this book.

Finally, I owe a great deal to Judith Leet for her professional editorial assistance and skill in finalizing and preparing the manuscript for publication.

Chapter 1

Harry Bingham Rises to the Occasion

On the eve of U.S. participation in World War II, Harry Bingham was helping to run an "underground railroad" in Marseilles, France, to smuggle Jews and non-Jews out of Europe before Hitler could capture and kill them. Bingham was then a U.S. vice consul stationed at Marseilles, in charge of issuing visas for the United States. Various estimates put the number of people Harry Bingham helped rescue from one thousand to two thousand—or even more. Bingham worked with an underground of French partisans, a few Americans, and others, and issued visas to desperate refugees who were prohibited from receiving them under State Department rules.

He often held planning meetings at his villa in Marseilles, and on occasion he even used his residence as a "halfway house" to hide refugees who, according to German-controlled French law at the time, should have been turned over to the Germans. It is a gripping tale of Bingham and others setting regard for other human lives above their own personal interests or their careers.

But it is also a story of a perilous adventure that turned Bingham's hair white. In early 1940, before this period started, it was reddish brown; when he returned home on leave fourteen months later, it was almost completely white. He was obviously stressed and very scared about the whole venture and what it might do to him personally. And his actions brought about what he feared most: he wasn't promoted and felt he had to resign from his chosen career at the Foreign Service in 1945. More than fifty years later, the U.S. government was willing to admit Bingham had made the right choice—that his dissent was "constructive." But by this time, Bingham had died.

Such is the story in general terms. The problem is we do not yet know all the details because they are emerging even as these pages are written. The facts are still being unearthed by the Bingham family, by scholars from such places as the U.S. Holocaust Museum, by Eric Saul of the Simon Wiesenthal Center, who was the creator of "Visas for Life" exhibit, and by others.

This research is all the more difficult because Bingham and the others in this mission to save lives were doing their best to hide their activities from others. And for reasons we still do not fully understand—perhaps the stress of it, or the strong opposition of their governments—they shared very little of their experiences, even long after the war was over. Perhaps Harry Bingham

Refugees lined up outside Harry Bingham's Marseilles consulate, circa 1940.

was haunted by all those long lines of people, waiting in front of his Marseilles consulate, whom he could not rescue. However, enough documentation has emerged to give a good idea of what Harry Bingham was up to.

Just Before America Entered World War II

To understand what Bingham did, it helps to understand the context in which he operated. At age thirty-four, he was posted to Marseilles in 1937. By 1940, Hitler had defeated France and divided the country into two zones, a Nazi-occupied zone in the north administered from Paris, and a theoretically French zone in the south (but still heavily influenced by the Germans) administered from Vichy. Among the orders and laws for governing France, the Germans issued one called Article 19, the "surrender on demand" document, stating any German prisoners in France had to be surrendered on demand. It said, among other things: "The French Government is obliged to surrender upon demand, all Germans named by the German Government in France, as well as in French possessions, Colonies, Protectorates, Territories and Mandates. . . . The French Government binds itself to prevent removal of German war and civil prisoners from France . . . into foreign countries."

Another point to remember is the U.S. State Department policy in 1940. At that time, the United States was not involved in the war and was trying to maintain—at least on the surface—neutral relations with Germany. This was one reason the State Department had a policy of not helping people evade the Germans. A telegram to this effect was issued by U.S. Secretary of State Cordell Hull on September 18, 1940, to the American Embassy in Vichy, forbidding such activities. It said, in part: "While Department is sympathetic with the plight of unfortunate refugees . . . this Government can not repeat not countenance activities . . . evading the laws of countries with which the United States maintains friendly relations." Cordell Hull had been appointed Secretary of State by Franklin Delano Roosevelt in 1933, serving at that post for eleven years until 1944; earlier he had served in the House and the Senate for almost twenty-five years.

Another consideration that factored into the State Department policy was anti-Semitism. As many documents from that era show, Nazi Germany was not the only country guilty of anti-Semitism; we had it in this country to some extent, too. For this reason, and because our government didn't want too many foreign refugees coming to the United States and taking jobs from Americans, especially during the Great Depression, it issued regulations severely limiting the number of Jews permitted to enter America.

Much later, Bingham summarized the net result of these factors, in an interview taped in 1980 by his granddaughter Tiffany Mitchell Bingham: "My boss who was the Consul General at that time, said, 'The Germans are going to win the war. Why should we do anything to offend them?' And he didn't want to give any visas to 'these Jewish people.'"

Finally, although that restriction was the official U.S. policy, there also seems to have been an unofficial policy that was quite different. Noted for her activism, Eleanor Roosevelt is known to have convinced her husband, Franklin Delano Roosevelt, that special exceptions in immigration policy should be made for certain Jewish artists and intellectuals living in Nazi-occupied Europe. Furthermore, she even gave her blessing to an organization founded to help these people escape, called the Emergency Rescue Committee (ERC). The Committee compiled a list of people to be rescued and sent a man named Varian Fry to Europe to oversee the effort. Then in his early thirties, Varian Fry was a graduate of Harvard and a New York journalist; since he spoke many languages and felt at home in Europe, the Committee thought he was the appropriate man for rescuing the noted

Women and children in an internment camp in France, circa 1940.

refugees on the list. Ironically, later on, the Emergency Rescue Committee essentially fired Fry because he—with Bingham's help—was adding many more names to the list and using procedures the ERC had not authorized.

The Visas Harry Bingham Signed in Marseilles

When Bingham was assigned as a vice consul at Marseilles in 1937, he was allowed to bring his growing family with him. He was eager for the assignment; he thought of it as a step up in his career. But then as war clouds gathered in 1940, his wife Rose and their four children (with another on the way) were evacuated to her family's home in Waycross, Georgia. From the day Rose left, until their reunion fourteen months later, he wrote scores of letters to her, expressing his sorrow at being apart from his family.

At the office, as vice consul, Bingham was in charge of issuing visas, both normal visas and emergency visas. Before 1940, anyone coming to the United States had to come in under the normal visas, and those visas were subject to rigorous and, as we have noted, anti-Semitic criteria. As we'll see later, Bingham stretched those criteria to save lives.

After 1940, a special emergency visa was created for an initial 2,500 people on the ERC list, although subsequently more names were added to the list. Those visas waived the normal criteria in order to expedite getting selected persons out of Europe—those who faced retribution from the Nazis. Bingham also violated laws in dealing with these kinds of emergency visas.

Varian Fry and Harry Bingham

Varian Fry is, to date, the American most celebrated for helping Jews escape Europe during World War II. He is the only American to receive the designation "Righteous Among the Nations" from Yad Vashem, the official Israeli government Holocaust remembrance agency. (At this writing, Bingham has been nominated for this award, and he has been given a special commendation from Yad Vashem.) Fry wrote a book about his exploits, *Surrender on Demand* (1945), that discusses Bingham in several places.

When Varian Fry arrived in Marseilles in 1940, Bingham was already there, helping people escape the Nazis by bending the rules regarding normal visas. Subsequently, Fry worked closely with Harry, exclusively on the matter of emergency visas, and Bingham added Fry to a network of escape facilitators that Bingham had already been using.

Moreover, according to Elizabeth Berman, former Research Curator of the Varian Fry exhibit at the U.S. Holocaust Museum and author of several magazine articles about Fry, Bingham on many occasions had traveled around France with Fry to contact people on the emergency list of names, whom Fry was trying to rescue.

Striking evidence that the two worked very closely together is Fry's hand-written inscription in a copy of his memoir (*Surrender on Demand*) that he presented to Bingham: "To my partner in the crime of saving human lives."

Years after the war, Fry, who also lived in Connecticut, visited Bingham's family at the Mumford House in Salem, Connecticut. Fry also was an accomplished photographer; he created a number of large brown-and-white photographs of us children, walking and playing in the fields and on the stone bridge across the brook, climbing on stone walls, and playing with our pets. These lovely photographs adorned the highboys and mantelpieces in our house for years to come.

On June 25, 2003, Elizabeth Berman summarized the importance of Harry Bingham to Varian Fry's mission for the Emergency Rescue Committee, describing the relationship between Fry and Bingham as follows:

Without Harry Bingham, Varian Fry's work would have been completely stymied. Fry needed someone at the Consulate to facilitate issuing visas and to help track down all the people on the Emergency list. Harry Bingham not only issued visas and helped find the people, he also harbored some of the people on the Emergency list in his home.

Bingham Visits French Concentration Camps

As part of his work in Marseilles, from November 27 to December 1, 1940, Bingham visited five French concentration camps in the Marseilles consular district, namely at Gurs, Vernet, Argeles-sur-Mer, Agde, and Les Milles. (His report about the trip was discovered over sixty years later in the Mumford House in 2003.) There were scores of these camps in France, originally created to deal with the influx of refugees from the Spanish

Varian Fry looks over European countryside, circa 1940. Fry later inscribed in a copy of his memoirs he sent to Bingham, "To my partner in the crime of saving human lives."

Civil War. The Vichy government used them as "transit camps," collection points for persons destined to be sent either to the more dangerous concentration camps in Germany and eastern Europe, or elsewhere.

Harry Bingham's report describes intolerable conditions: a lack of heating in the camps; large numbers of old men, women, and children; very bad food; primitive outhouses a long distance (fifty to one hundred yards) from the main dwellings; insufficient bedding; barracks infested with rats, mice, and lice; hostile attendants; very serious health problems—and hundreds of deaths. During these days in the early 1940s, the U.S. Consulate in Marseilles was receiving four hundred letters a day from these camp inmates seeking visas to the United States.

Chapter 2

The Rescue of Lion Feuchtwanger

The Lion Feuchtwanger case is a well-documented example of Bingham's collaboration with Varian Fry of the Emergency Rescue Committee (ERC). In the summer of 1940, Varian Fry arrived in Marseilles, and Fry and Bingham began to cooperate on the ERC list and to help designated artists, writers, intellectuals, and others—to escape the Nazis with emergency visas. In brief, Bingham and a few trusted colleagues helped Lion Feuchtwanger, who was wanted as an anti-Nazi writer, escape from a French concentration camp at Nîmes, disguised in a woman's clothing— in shawl, blanket, and dark glasses.

And Bingham hid Lion, still in disguise, for over a month in his own villa in Marseilles, until he could escape to freedom and America. To account for Lion's presence at the villa, Bingham explained his mother-in-law was visiting from Waycross, Georgia.

As Lion described in his diary (see Appendix 4), he was taken completely by surprise while at the authorized swimming hole and whisked away from the concentration camp at Nîmes by "an elegant diplomatic auto," and was not even allowed to bring his bag, his sole possession, which was abandoned at the camp. To be persuaded to let the Americans "abduct" him on the spot, Lion was told he could possibly escape from France by a Red Cross ship. The diplomatic car was frequently stopped and searched by police en route to Bingham's villa at Marseilles. "We are checked once again by police, but everything goes all right," Lion described the frightening trip.

Lion wanted to avoid any German-controlled police because he was on Hitler's "most wanted" list of enemies. Born in Munich, Germany, in 1884, to Jewish parents, he had earned a doctorate in philology and literature in 1918 in German universities. In Germany, he had published his first historical novel in 1923 (*The Ugly Duchess*) and published another historical novel in 1925, about a Jewish financier in eighteenth-century Germany, titled *Jew Suss*.

But his next book, a contemporary novel, *The Oppermanns*, plunged him into serious trouble with the Nazis; it told about what happened to a Jewish family under Hitler. After the novel's publication in 1933, he was quickly exiled from Germany that same year, and settled in Sanary, France, for the next seven years. By 1940, he was forced into the concentration camp in Nîmes—

until Bingham and Fry plotted to rescue him.

After the escape car made it to Bingham's villa safely, Lion continued to record in his diary what happened to him and Bingham daily. The very night he reached Bingham's villa, he was disappointed: "it turns out the story with the Red Cross [a ship to escape from France] will in no way be simple. The good-natured, embarrassed Bingham gradually explains to me the several details about the escape plan that do not sound very promising." Often recording his physical ailments in the diary, he revealed the intense pressure he felt under: "I am bothered by stomach ache, headache, and general weakness."

Lion, from his own perspective, described Bingham as he appeared that summer of 1940: "an awkward, friendly, puritanical, dutiful, somewhat sad New Englander, who is very attached to his wife." Noting that Harry missed his wife and children very much, who had been sent to America for safekeeping, Lion suggests that the absence of his family might explain his sadness. Or we may now conjecture that his sadness might have also been caused by the daily, lengthy lines of people waiting in front of his Marseilles consulate and pleading for visas—and Bingham was not able to provide visas for an unknown number of them. His sadness might also have been caused by his disagreements with his immediate superior, who was confident the Germans would win the war, but Bingham could not go along with the Nazis or their inhuman treatment of people.

Lion recognized that Harry felt under intense pressure at the consulate—disagreeing with his superiors about the rules for issuing visas. "Bingham tells about all the work that emigrants are making him. He is always tired and exhausted." About a week

Bingham's residence in Marseilles, circa 1939.

later, when they were talking together, Harry received a phone call from his superior, the consul general, "which puts him into a sharp conversation . . . he is totally troubled, and I fear that my own thing will be unfavorably influenced."

Bingham confides in Lion: "He explains very confidentially about his difficult position in the Consulate, and our personal relations improve." Lion is not the only refugee hiding in Bingham's villa; a certain Joachim is also hiding at the same time.

Bingham, worrying about his presence, tells Lion that he should leave the villa quite soon: "he fears that it will be too dangerous for him if I stay too long in his house." But Bingham later that same evening changes his mind, quiets his own fears, and then urges Lion to stay longer.

Golo Mann, Thomas Mann's son, is the only one of Lion's friends who is supposed to know that Lion is hiding in the villa. Trusted friends at Bingham's villa suggest many escape plans for Lion to use, but they are ruled out as too risky. Various schemes are discussed—by hiring a ship to smuggle him out, by flying him to Portugal, by giving him false documents—and their chances of succeeding.

These actions of Bingham—hiding Lion in his villa and not turning him over to the police—were in clear violation of Article 19 (that Germany's most-wanted enemies had to be surrendered to the police). During Lion's stay, Bingham also issued him one of the emergency visas to enter the United States. Although this may have been in accordance with State Department rules, the fact that Harry issued it under an assumed name—under a Mr. Wetcheek—was not (Feuchtwanger means "wet cheek" in German).

By August 12, Lion notes: "The prospect of escape lifts my

mood, but the impending hardships and dangers make me nervous." Two weeks later, Bingham is in "a bad mood," and Lion isn't sleeping. "Big panic" takes place—about what to do if someone comes to Bingham enquiring about a Mr. Wetcheek. Lion records "a lot of unpleasant little things to think about." Lion's diary suggests how both Bingham and Lion are anguished over these summer weeks of 1940. Lion is still sleeping badly; the various plans for his escape do not materialize.

Toward the end of his stay, late August, Lion notes that Varian Fry and Heinrich Mann (the brother of Thomas Mann and a distinguished writer in his own right) come to dinner at the villa. Hoping to flee from the Germans, Heinrich Mann complains that one of the plans of a boat is not going to work—and "will never work." At that same dinner, Varian Fry proposes a plan that Lion agrees to without hesitation: "we should under his [Fry's] protection simply go over the Spanish border illegally. The plan immediately takes shape, and I quickly agree without delay. A lot of individual technical difficulties, but I am in a good mood because there is a tangible plan." Varian Fry's plan works out safely, and Lion is at last rescued.

Feuchtwanger's wife, Marta, accompanied him; she crossed the border into Spain following Harry Bingham's advice to trick the guards. She threw packs of Camel cigarettes on the table in front of the border guards—to distract them from scrutinizing her papers. Harry had placed these packs of cigarettes in her backpack. She later wrote that Harry's advice had worked like a charm, and she ran down the mountain into Spain as fast as she could.

After getting past Spanish officials and safely aboard the S.S. *Excalibur*, Feuchtwanger sent Bingham a thank-you note as he was steaming for America. In 2003, Bingham's daughter Abigail and her husband Bill Endicott discovered this long-lost letter in the Mumford House, written in Feuchtwanger's tortured English (next page):

Bingham's diplomatic identification, 1940.

American Export Lines
On Board
S. S. EXCALIBUR
28th Sept. [1940]

My dear Harry Bingham,
Well, here I am, I cannot believe it yet. Now, I should have to write a nice letter full of thanks, but I will not, I think, it does not need, you know exactly what I am feeling for you. Let me only repeat that it was a great chance that it was not Mr. X or Mr. Y, in whose house I had to face these bad days, but yours. I ever shall remember with pleasure those some good talks we had.

hope to see you

When you will get this letter, you certainly will be informed how all happened. It was a great stress all at all, I feel a little exhausted, I miss my things, I have only this famous rucksack, but I feel happy.

Well, I hope to see you soon in America, and
meantimes, I should be glad to hear from you.
For your stay in Europe have a so good time as
possible, give my greetings to Elisabeth and Fanny
and have sometimes a friendly thought of mine

Yours for ever,

Wetcheek

SOON in America

Lion characterizes his stay at the villa as "these bad days," but is very grateful he spent those bad days in Bingham's company. And he wittily signs his name Wetcheek.

Even as the Feuchtwanger case was unfolding, U.S. Secretary of State Cordell Hull on September 18, 1940, issued a telegram to the American Embassy in Vichy, condemning such activities. The telegram read in part:

You should inform . . . Mr. Fry in personal interview that while Department is sympathetic to the plight of unfortunate refugees . . . this government can not repeat not countenance the activities as reported of . . . Mr. Fry and other persons, however well-meaning their motives may be, in carrying on activities evading the laws of countries with which the United States maintains friendly relations.

This was a warning not only to Fry but to Bingham himself. Within a short period of time, both were removed from their positions in Marseilles, Bingham transferred to Lisbon and Fry removed from his position at the ERC.

After Lion escaped to America, he quickly published, in 1941, *The Devil in France*—a memoir based on his diaries—on his experience of escaping the Nazis, crediting Bingham with much help for his survival. Varian Fry's book, *Surrender on Demand* (1945), also discussed Bingham's indispensable help in the Marseilles consulate.

Hiram Bingham IV looks over Marseilles harbor, circa 1940.

Chapter 3

Visas for Marc Chagall, Thomas Mann's Brother and Son, and Many Others

In addition to Lion Feuchtwanger, Harry Bingham issued emergency visas to other prominent artists, intellectuals, and writers. Among those he helped to rescue from the Nazis were well-known painter Marc Chagall and his wife Bella.

Chagall was born in 1887 in Vitebsk in the Russian Empire to Jewish parents, and in 1907 he went to St. Petersburg to study art—for a time with Leon Bakst. In 1910, he joined other avant-garde painters who had flocked to Paris, then the center of the art world.

His fanciful paintings, including *I and the Village*, *The Fiddler*, *Paris Through the Window*, and *Jew in Green*, are now in major museums and collections of the world. In 1915, he married Bella Rosenfeld, the daughter of a Vitebsk merchant, and she appeared in many of his paintings, including *Double Portrait with a Glass of Wine*. During the rise of the Nazis, the Chagalls moved from Paris to more southern locations in France and eventually, in July 1941, fled to America—with assistance by Varian Fry and Harry Bingham.

In 1941, Chagall wrote a handwritten note to Bingham, thanking him after a visit Bingham made to the Chagalls' home, probably to plan their leaving France. Chagall wrote in part:

Thank you with all our hearts. We had a great deal of pleasure in spending these last two days with you.

Moving Chagall and his wife out of the sphere of the Nazis suggests the dangers to Varian Fry and Harry Bingham. The Chagalls, Fry, and Bingham came together in Harry's villa to plot how to rescue the Chagalls. Fry and Bingham shortly later brought the couple to the U.S. Consulate in Marseilles, where Bingham promptly gave them visas, although the couple did not have the affidavits required by the State Department.

In the spring of 1941, just before the couple was about to flee from Marseilles, Chagall was snared in a police roundup of Jews. With boldness, threats, and cajoling, Fry and Bingham somehow persuaded the police to release him. The Chagalls reached Lisbon—on the way to America—on May 11, 1941.

Many years later, in May 2006, Marc Chagall's granddaughter, Dr. Bella Meyer, spoke at a public "Celebration in Honor of the

Diplomat's Battle to Save Jews Emerges

A 1941 photo, showing (left to right) Varian Fry, Marc Chagall, Bella Chagall, and Hiram Bingham, standing behind Bella Chagall (from the New York Times*).*

Hiram Bingham IV U.S. Postage Stamp," in Washington, D.C. In her speech, she recalled sitting on her grandfather's knee when she was a little girl, while he told her many stories, including the one about his rescue from the Nazis in Marseilles with the help of Bingham and Fry. She emphasized how grateful she and her grandfather have always been to Harry Bingham, for helping Chagall and his wife, Bella, escape to freedom. She also said that Hiram Bingham IV and Marc Chagall were two men of vision, and because of Hiram Bingham IV, her grandfather Chagall, a man whose vision was of "freedom, love, and passion," was able to continue his work—his stained glass and his painting—in the world.

Harry Bingham also issued emergency visas to Thomas Mann's son, Golo Mann, a historian, and to Thomas Mann's brother, Heinrich Mann, also a novelist. Thomas Mann, winner of the Nobel Prize in Literature in 1929, wrote Bingham a letter of appreciation for his rescuing of many individuals, in general, and his son and his brother, in particular:

I want particularly to be able to thank you personally for your sympathetic help to the many men and women, including members of my own family, who have turned to you for assistance.

Bingham and Varian Fry used the expression "Harry's friends" to signify those people on the Emergency Rescue Committee list. Along with other trusted members of the French resistance, they met at Bingham's villa on the Rue de Roland to plan the needed visas, affidavits, complicated papers required by France, Spain, Portugal, and the United States; they also planned escape routes and the most expedient time for the flight. The prominent artists they helped escape included Marcel Duchamp, Jacques Lipchitz, André Masson, Max Ernst, as well as the poet André Breton. They also helped Franz Werfel, author of *The Song of Bernadette*, and his wife, the widow of Gustav Mahler.

Fry and Bingham also aided Otto Meyerhof, winner of the Nobel Prize in physics, and his family. They also rescued anti-Nazi politicians, lawyers, and other opponents of Hitler, including Konrad Heiden, an anti-Hitler biographer. Fry, Bingham, and the ERC were able to rescue more than 2,500 people who otherwise would have been murdered in the Holocaust.

When Fry heard his partner at the Marseilles consulate was reassigned in May 1941, he was rightly upset at the idea of Bingham moving to Lisbon. And Fry shortly afterwards lost his job for the Emergency Rescue Committee—probably for adding more people to the ERC list of names.

An Anti-Nazi Family

In addition to collaborating with Varian Fry and providing emergency visas for his list, Bingham continued, as part of his responsibility as vice consul, to issue regular visas. And he stretched the rules there too. The case of the Winkler family is a good example—one of the cases that has recently come to light. On November 16, 2003, Lilian Winkler Stuart Smith recorded the story of what had happened to her family (in a taped interview made by Bingham's daughter Abigail, and William Endicott, Abigail's husband, at their home in Bethesda, Maryland). By sheer chance, Lilian had actually met Bingham at a Groton School parents' weekend a half century after he saved her life.

Lilian was the daughter of Paul Winkler, the publisher and owner of a newspaper syndicate in Paris. His papers had printed anti-Nazi material, and these articles had put him on the Gestapo "wanted" list—even though he himself was not Jewish.

Realizing that he and his family had to escape the Nazis, Winkler went south to Lyon in late 1940 to search for visas for America. He had carried on business relations in America and even had maintained an office in New York, so he could point out he wasn't going to be a charge on the American government. But as Lilian, sixteen at the time, recounts it, the American consul in Lyon said to Winkler:

"Yes, I'll give you a visa, a visitor's visa, but you must leave two of your children here because we want to make sure that you are not going to over-stay your visitor's visa." And my father said, "Not on your life! I'm not going to leave two of my children back here!" So, he decided to go to Marseilles, where he also had business dealings and tried the American consulate there. This time he ran into Harry, who was willing to issue visas to the whole family, in violation of State Department regulations.

Lilian then described the harrowing journey that she and her fourteen-year-old brother made from Bordeaux to Lyon and then on to Marseilles to pick up their visas from Harry Bingham; they had not actually been with their father when he had first met with

Harry. At that time, they needed a German pass to make such a trip because it entailed crossing the border between German-occupied France and Vichy France. And there was no way Lilian and her brother would be given such passes.

So Paul Winkler arranged to have an associate sneak back to Bordeaux to fetch his children, by going through an estate with a forest, situated right on the borderline between German-occupied France and Vichy France, by dodging German sentries, and by continuing on his way to Bordeaux where the children were waiting.

Even though the Germans had generally stopped travel to Vichy France, trains remained for people involved in the Vichy government to get from one place to another. The plan was for Paul's associate to take Lilian and her brother on such a train, get off at the appropriate stop, and sneak through the woods at the estate again, thus making it across the border:

We got on the train, we got to the frontier. And on board the train came a German soldier, accompanied by a young man who was Alsatian, who was his translator. And the man who was taking us through persuaded this young man to persuade the German to let us through. He said, "Look, these are just two poor young children. Their parents are on the other side. They've been separated from their parents. Let them go." And this young Alsatian persuaded this German to let us through. So, we've been very lucky in our lives.

While Lilian and her brother were allowed to go across the border legally, their father's associate, who was accompanying them, had to sneak through the forest of the estate again.

After that, Lilian and her brother made it to Lyon and finally to Marseilles, where they went to the American consulate and received the visas Harry had promised them. She remembers, in going to the American consulate in Marseilles, that the building was "under siege" with all the people trying to get visas to get out of France.

Cases Recently Discovered

After several survivors (or members of their family) had seen the stamp-campaign website, which I started about Bingham's activities in Marseilles, a number of them wrote me, describing cases that they had personally been involved in. One such case was that of Pierre Shostal, who sent in a statement from his Jewish father, Walter Shostal, who was formerly a member of the French Foreign Legion. Walter Shostal had tried to obtain visas for himself and his family to escape to America but, like the Winklers, did not succeed until he met Bingham.

A similar letter came from Rabbi Joseph Schachter. He wrote that he and his entire family (six people in all) "received the life-saving visas, dated Feb. 7, 1941," from Bingham—and even had saved the original visas signed by Bingham—to verify that Harry Bingham was the man responsible for rescuing them.

Yet another letter to me was from Ralph Hockley:

Life-saving family visa issued by Harry Bingham in 1941.

AFFIDAVIT IN LIEU OF

PASSPORT

Republic of France
Department of Bouches du Rhône }
City of Marseille } ss.
Consulate of the United States }
    of America }

BEFORE me, Hiram Bingham Jr., Vice Consul of the United States
America at Marseille, France, duly commissioned and qualified,
personally appeared Salomon SCHACHTER who, being duly sworn according
law, deposes and says:

That his full and true name is Salomon SCHACHTER,

That he resides at Marseille, France, 33 rue des Dominicaines

That he was born on October 3rd 1898 at Crakovie, Poland

That he is accompanied by his children : Josef, Dorothea and
Adelaide SCHACHTER.

That he has lost his Polish nationality and is unable to obtain
a valid travel document on account of conditions prevailing in France
at the present time.

And further deponent saith not.

Hiram Bingham IV, circa 1980.

Salomon SCHACHTER

Subscribed and sworn to before me this 3rd day of February 1941.

Hiram Bingham Jr.
Vice Consul of the United States
    of America

Service No. 971
No Fee Prescribed.

Affidavit in lieu of passport, 1941, signed by Harry Bingham.

I could write a treatise about what Consul Hiram Bingham did to save refugees. . . . He definitely helped to save my life and that of my parents and sister.

And later, in commemoration of Harry's hundredth birthday, he wrote again:

I have just explained to my sister's nineteen-year-old grandson that without your father [Harry Bingham], he probably would never have been born. What more can I say?

Among documents found after Bingham's death was this particularly moving letter of thanks from Fred Altman to Bingham, dated February 28, 1941, which says, in part:

In my prayers your person took shape, and my heart is so full now that I think I must write you. . . . My heart skipped a beat when you gave me my chance. It means Life, Future, Ideals. . . . I feel overwhelmed by this kindness.

Another currently living survivor, an eighty-year-old California woman, Elly Sherman, sent me the following emotional e-mail in October 2005:

Of the three in my family [your father] saved . . . I am the last one alive and I write this with trembling fingers and many a tear.

I am the last one alive

[Your father] provided us with [documents] because we no longer held citizenship in any country, and therefore had no papers. . . . I still have the document. We cannot honor him enough.

[He] saved my Mother, my sister, and [me]. Without him we would not have been able to avoid the concentration camp to which we were assigned two days later.

—Elly Sherman

How many people did Bingham save altogether? No one really knows the exact number, for new cases are still emerging. And we assume that many other cases—the evidence has disappeared over time—will never be known. But Friedrich B. Heine, a representative in France in 1940 for the German Social-Democrat party, a newspaper editor, and an anti-Hitler activist, wrote Harry Bingham a letter on April 28, 1985, saying, in part:

Most probably you will not remember me: in 1940 I had been in Marseilles, and there had the good fortune to meet you quite a few times. Thanks to you and your understanding of the situation, probably more than 1,000 refugees have been saved. I am now over eighty years of age, and the events I refer to are known to very few people nowadays—but I still have the memory of those days and of your so very great help.

Chapter 4

The Price of Harry Bingham's Dissent

Varian Fry had worked well with Bingham, arranging for many to flee the Nazis. No wonder, then, when he heard that Bingham was going to be reassigned to Lisbon, Varian Fry expressed his displeasure:

Wednesday, May 7, 1941 Harry Bingham told me this morning that he has just received instructions to go to Lisbon. He is closing his house and packing his things. His going will be a great loss to the refugees, and may seriously cripple our work.

He had been the one man at the Consulate who had always seemed to understand that his job now is not to apply the rules rigidly but to save lives whenever he could. His behavior has always been in sharp contrast to that of most other American Consuls in France. I hate to think what it is going to be like here after he has gone.

After Harry Bingham did leave for Lisbon, Fry complained about his replacement:

The new man in charge of visas at the Marseille Consulate is young and inexperienced. This is his first post. Afraid of making mistakes, he tries to solve his problems by refusing visas whenever he can. But he is also a snob. The other day I talked to him about just two cases, both women. One was a German Social Democratic underground worker. She had a good affidavit. The other was the Countess X. She has no affidavit at all. B—— refused to give a visa to the German political refugee. "How do I know she won't do underground work in the United States if I let her in?" he asked. But when I mentioned the Countess X he became

sweet as honey. "Oh, I'm sure there'll be no diffi-
culty about her visa," he said. "Just tell her to
come in any time she wants to and ask to see me
personally. I'll fix her up right away." He didn't
even ask what the Countess's politics were. She got
her visa the next day.

Harry Bingham's Conversation Taped by His Granddaughter

The following audiotape, made around 1980 by Bingham's
teen-aged granddaughter Tiffany (who interviewed him for a Salem,
Connecticut, school class project), reveals that Bingham issued "as
many visas as I could" when he was in Marseilles:

Bingham: We were transferred in 1937 to Marseilles in France
where there were a great many refugees from Nazi Germany
trying to get visas to get to the United States, and part of my work
was giving visas to these refugees. . . . They [the Germans] had a
lot of what was called the Fifth Column, which were sort of spies
and people living in southern France. And we got rumors that
the Germans were going to come down to southern France and
would be there any time. . . . Although we were not in the war,
most of our government was on the side of the allies, the British
and the French. But my [superior] said, "The Germans are going
to win the war. Why should we do anything to offend them?"
And he didn't want to give any visas to "these Jewish people."

So . . . I had to do as much as I could. . . . The Germans had signed an agreement with the French that they could stay in that zone, but they must surrender any Germans that were there— any refugees—on demand, and they would then be sent back to concentration camps in Germany.

Granddaughter: What was the most important thing that you did for the Jews?

Bingham: Well, in a way, it was getting as many visas as I could to as many people. And we did help.

And Harry eventually paid a price for the numbers of visas he issued in Marseilles. His actions were not approved by his superiors, including the Secretary of State Cordell Hull in Washington, D. C., who had criticized Varian Fry by name in his cablegram of September 1940.

Reassigned to Buenos Aires

While Bingham posthumously has been recognized for his efforts against the Nazis in Marseilles, few people realize that he kept up this fight in Buenos Aires when he was stationed there, following his years in Marseilles (with a brief stint in Lisbon between).

On July 15, 2003, Abigail and Bill Endicott found a number of records in the basement of the Mumford House that tell the story of the Buenos Aires period, at least in outline. In fact, much of it can be told in Harry's own words, for he kept surprisingly detailed notes (in the form of long typed diary entries) and saved many pertinent documents.

From May to August, 1941, Bingham was reassigned temporarily to Lisbon because the State Department needed his expertise in visas—to handle a flood of applicants there. This flood came about because, in the spring of 1941, the French government started issuing exit visas. The many people who wanted to leave France could now do so legally, and they sought to do it through Lisbon. Then in September 1941, he was moved from Europe to South America; after a brief home leave in the United States, Harry Bingham and his family went to Buenos Aires in October of 1941. The reason for his reassignment is a matter of conjecture, but at that time many American officials in the State Department and the Foreign Service opposed the issuing of visas to refugees fleeing the Nazis.

Once in Buenos Aires, for several years until 1944, Bingham's notes and records appear to relate only to the routine cases that he handled and to routine descriptions of daily life with the family. But starting in 1944, several things happened that would eventually lead to Bingham resigning from the State Department.

The first problem was that Bingham was experiencing increasing frustration with the U.S. government for not taking a harder line against Fascists in Argentina. In a number of memoranda, some of which were clearly sent to higher officials, Bingham argued in increasingly strong terms that the United States should send military personnel to Argentina to root out the Nazis there. Typical was this statement: "Perón [president of Argentina] and his whole gang are completely unreliable, and whatever happens, all countries in South America will be seed-

*Applicants for visas line up outside the American consulate
in Marseilles, circa 1940.*

beds of Nazism after the war. Constant vigilance will be required to weed out dangerous elements for years to come."

The second problem was that Bingham was getting passed over for promotion.

Resignation

In a 1945 diary entry, Bingham complained that 150 Foreign Service officers had passed him on the promotion ladder. On May 15, 1945, he wrote a diary entry in uncharacteristically harsh words about the situation:

PROMOTIONS! . . . but not for me . . . hell! . . . it doesn't matter but it does damn, d— d—. . . career again blasted . . . why? What's the matter?. . . who's responsible?. . .why are these others jumped ahead? . . . R says it's the price for doing what I want instead of what they want . . . no real change . . . but terribly discouraging . . . Ed says he doesn't know why and that it can't be my efficiency report from here . . . he says he will make inquiries in Washington.

There is no record that these "inquiries" ever produced an adequate explanation. In this entry, he refers to his career "again" blasted. He is aware of a prior time his career was blocked; we may intimate he is referring to the loss of his position as the vice consul at Marseilles.

Two days after the 1945 diary entry, Bingham was talking

about getting out of the State Department and doing something else. Later that year, he resigned. His years in Argentina had added to his nonconformist reputation and sealed his fate. He had acted and spoken his conscience, and the price for that was being passed over and left with no alternative but to leave.

After resigning from the Foreign Service in 1945, Bingham brought Rose and his family to his ancestral home in Salem, Connecticut, where they raised their eleven children and he lived out the remaining forty-two years of his life.

Bingham never boasted of his heroic activities during the nightmare of the Holocaust. Consequently, his children never knew the extent of his rescue efforts until recent years, when long dormant documents were discovered in museums and in Harry Bingham's Connecticut farmhouse.

Chapter 5

Harry Bingham's Private Life

Harry Bingham was the second of seven sons of explorer Hiram Bingham III (1875–1956), who is best known for discovering and excavating the Inca ruins in Machu Picchu in Peru, and later served as a governor of Connecticut and as a U.S. Senator. Harry's great-grandfather and grandfather, Hiram Bingham I and Hiram Bingham II, were pioneer missionaries in the Hawaiian and Gilbertese Islands during the nineteenth century. These soldiers of their faith both influenced the course of history in those territories and set a moral compass for their descendant, Hiram Bingham IV.

Hiram Bingham III, Harry Bingham IV's celebrated father, circa 1916.
Hiram Bingham III was son and grandson of missionaries in the Pacific Sandwich and
Gilbert Islands, an explorer who excavated Inca ruins at Machu Picchu, aviator,
professor at Yale, governor from Connecticut, and U.S. Senator.

Rose Lawton Morrison prepares to be presented to King George V and Queen Mary in London, 1934.

Harry Bingham's mother, Alfreda Mitchell (1874–1967), was the granddaughter of Charles Tiffany, who founded Tiffany and Company. His mother's uncle was Louis Comfort Tiffany, well known for his museum-quality designs, glassware, and stained glass windows.

Harry Bingham was educated at Groton, as were all his brothers. At Groton, he learned that religion, by one definition, was "giving the best that you have to the best that you know," a motto he remembered all his life. A good student, doing well at math and sciences, he considered becoming a doctor; he was also a good athlete, excelling at gymnastics and soccer. Today, Groton's Director of Athletics has Harry Bingham's name and favorite motto on a plaque, displayed by the door of his office.

From Groton, he went to Yale, class of 1925; all of his brothers went to Yale, except Mitchell, who studied painting in Paris. At Yale, he studied math, religion, philosophy, and ethics. He recalled, at age eighty:

At Yale, I started to study science—math was my best subject, but when I asked what light, electricity, and gravity were, I was told that nobody really knew. "God knows!" they said—so I started [my] interest in religion, and my favorite course was by a professor of philosophy, Professor Bennett, who gave a course in ethics.

He continued his interest in gymnastics and soccer, and played soccer for the Yale team. From Yale, he taught at Indian

Mountain School (Connecticut) before entering Harvard Law School; but before he graduated from law school, he took the Foreign Service Exam, and did very well. Rather than finishing Harvard Law School, he decided to take a position with the U.S. Foreign Service. He served in Kobe, Japan, as a civilian secretary in the United States Embassy; he was also an aide to Ambassador Grew and helped write speeches for the ambassador.

Another assignment in the U.S. Foreign Service was in Beijing, China, as a foreign service officer. He served in the Far East for a total of four years. He was then assigned to Europe: he first served in Warsaw, Poland, sharing a flat with another diplomat, Charles W. Yost, whose daughter Felicity became Bingham's goddaughter. In 1934, Bingham was assigned as third secretary to the United States Embassy in London.

Also in London, he met his future wife, Rose Lawton Morrison, a college drama teacher from Waycross, Georgia.

Rose and Harry's Lifelong Romance

In London, one of Harry's assignments was to prepare the documents of young ladies being "presented to the Court of St. James," that is, debutantes being presented to King George V and Queen Mary. During these festivities, Bingham was chosen by the U.S. ambassador to represent him at a private dinner with Rose and her aunt Rose Douglas Lewis, wife of U.S. Senator James Hamilton Lewis of Illinois. It was on this occasion that Harry and Rose first danced together, after which—Rose later told her children—she wanted to dance with him for the rest of her life.

They saw each other only four times before Bingham followed her ship back to the United States to marry her in 1934

Above: Rose and Harry's growing family on flight from Argentina to Miami, Florida, just before he resigned from the Foreign Service, 1945.

Right: Harry and Rose's budding family in Marseilles. Left to right: Tiffany, John, Rose, Hiram ("Tony"), Thomas, circa 1939.

and brought her back to London with him. They both loved children and so, in time, they had eleven. Six were born abroad while Bingham served in foreign posts, and five were born in the United States. From London, Bingham and Rose were posted to Marseilles in 1937. By 1940, however, the situation had become so dangerous that they decided Rose and the children should return to the United States. Bingham remained alone in Marseilles another fourteen months. These months are the period of his "constructive dissent" when he obtained visas for people escaping from the Nazi regime. He was briefly posted in Lisbon, Portugal, before reuniting with his family in the United States.

By the time of their reunion in Waycross, Georgia, a new child had been born to the couple, and Harry's hair had turned completely white—perhaps from all the stress; Rose said she barely recognized him. Rose and Harry renewed their wedding vows after being reunited. Shortly thereafter, Harry was then assigned to Buenos Aires, Argentina, and he brought his family. The Bingham family arrived in Buenos Aires in October 1941.

Chapter 6

After the Foreign Service

After his resignation from the
Foreign Service in 1945, Bingham
retired to Salem, Connecticut, from
what had turned out to be his final
post in Buenos Aires, Argentina.
He began to engage in various business pursuits, such as real estate and
inventions. Among his inventions
was the "Sportatron," which was a
minigym—and the games and sports
to play within this minigym. During
his retirement, Bingham had both
ups—seeing his children get into
good schools through scholarships—
and downs—losing money on some
business transactions.

Perhaps he experienced feelings of isolation on his rural Connecticut farm, far from the affairs of state and of the world, which had been such a large part of his life for many years. However, if such was the case, he kept abreast of world and national affairs and did not show any outward discontentment to his family or friends.

In his spare time, Bingham loved to paint and copied the old masters, such as El Greco, to learn from them. Having met Chagall when he was vice consul in Marseilles, he admired Chagall's works greatly and would attempt to recreate them. He also attempted his own original paintings, including a painting of his homestead, Mumford House. He also encouraged and inspired his own children to paint.

Home in Salem, Connecticut

Rose and Harry raised their children in the Mumford House in Salem, Connecticut, built in 1769, and owned by Bingham's ancestor John Mumford. Mumford had managed the farm for its owner, William Brown, a wealthy Tory merchant from Salem, Massachusetts, who fled the colonies when the British lost the Revolutionary War. The Connecticut state legislature had then confiscated the abandoned estate and sold it to Mumford.

We eleven children were raised in this lovely rural setting beginning in 1946. Our mother used to joke that she would have been happy to have twelve children because they "would

Top right: Marc Chagall's stained glass windows, Jerusalem.

Bottom right: One of Bingham's paintings of his beloved homestead, the Mumford House, in Salem, Connecticut, inherited through a Tiffany family trust, painted circa 1948.

Harry Bingham displays his artwork, circa 1984.

Bingham studied how to paint by copying the old masters.

Bingham painted to music in his last years, creating imaginative and colorful works.

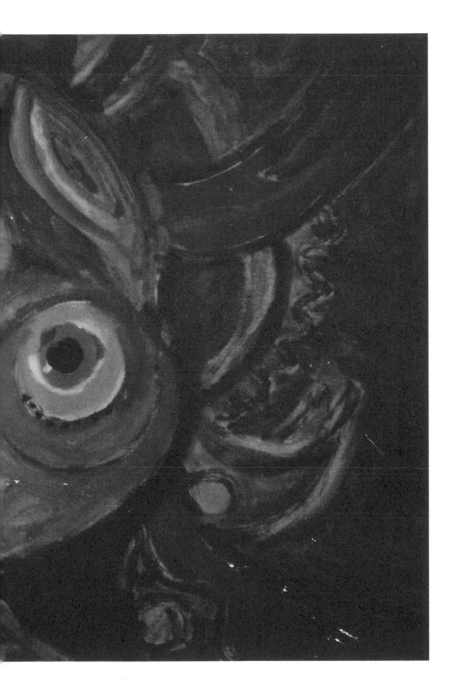

be cheaper by the dozen." The children were—from oldest to youngest—Tiffany, Hiram (Tony), Thomas, John, David, Robert Kim, Cecilia, Abigail, Margaret, G. Benjamin, and William.

Bingham spent countless hours with us inventing games and teaching us athletic skills. We learned to play modified sports in his Sportatron, and he hoped to mass market his invention. A hotel in Miami exhibited one minicourt for a year, as did a department store in New York City, Abercrombie and Fitch, which installed a Sportatron on its roof top—on a trial-run basis. We children enjoyed demonstrating Sportatron games to potential buyers—recreation and park managers, mayors, and other officials from neighboring towns. We would help load and unload heavy chain-link panels, transported on Bingham's large red company truck to demonstration sites.

One of Bingham's dreams was to install countless Sporta-trons on the roof tops of apartment buildings in crowded cities like New York and Tokyo, to give residents the opportunity to play sports "right upstairs." Some family and friends did purchase the bulky product. After seventeen years, his patent for the Sportatron expired, essentially bringing down the curtain on his marketing dream.

We children went off to boarding school at an early age. The seven boys attended Groton School in Groton, Massachusetts—the same school he had attended—and the four girls attended Miss Porter's School in Farmington, Connecticut. All attended college, though not everyone completed a degree.

Deep Moral Fiber

Bingham was a man of deep moral conviction. He and Rose raised their eleven children to be honest and compassionate, and to live by the golden rule. He often reminded us that there is a "spark of divinity in every human being" and that we should "do unto others" accordingly. One example of his moral strictness comes to mind: the greater Bingham family went to a beach in Waterford, Connecticut, where the youngsters were often attracted to an amusement park nearby at Ocean Beach—right across a tidal stream. When I was about six, we children walked along the beach to Ocean Beach, went to the arcade, rode the so-called Octopus, and played miniature golf. When we returned to our beach, Bingham was distraught to learn that we had not paid the three-cent admission fee for pedestrians (although we had paid for the rides and miniature golf). He scolded us: "You children are not worth more than the three cents you cheated the park out of." That really hurt.

Nevertheless, whenever my father would meet a perceived ethical violation by any of his children with an angry shout, his anger would fade away quickly, and he would become a loving being soon again.

Rose and Harry Kept a Loving Home

In a *New London Day* article, my wife Anne Carr Bingham recounted her first visit to the Mumford House in 1965, a few months before she and I were married:

Rose and Harry ready to go out on their fortieth wedding anniversary, September 8, 1974.

(Photo by their nephew, Dr. Russell N. Bingham.)

How vividly I recollect the first visit I made to my future husband's family for dinner. There were seven or eight of the 11 children gathered around a long table, one end of which was graced by their charming mother, the other end presided over by the family patriarch. Dinner began with a sung blessing, and proceeded with lively conversation. Love hovered over their table—by the end of the meal, I knew I must be part of that family forever. . . . Family mealtime: a sacramental custom to be cherished and perpetuated.

In his twilight years, Bingham loved to play the cello, and either Rose or one of the children accompanied him on the piano while many of those gathered sang along.

Memories of Harry Bingham

The Bingham family is rich in memories of Harry Bingham—whether as a beloved father or a grandfather or an uncle.

His oldest son, my brother Hiram A. (Tony) Bingham, remembers Harry as an enthusiastic philosopher, inventor, and Christian teacher:

He had a curious mind and was himself quite inventive. He created card games and sport games (Florball and others, using the curved racquet for

Rose and Harry's family, circa 1953. Standing (left to right), Cecilia, David, Tony, John, Thomas, Abigail, Robert Kim; seated (left to right), Tiffany, Margaret, Rose, Harry, Benjamin.

what is a family?

Bingham family gathers for Christmas dinner

A custom to cherish

Bingham family gathers for Christmas dinner (from New London Day).

THE ROSE ANU HIRAM BINGHAM GRANDSONS AND GREAT GRANDSONS!

(Missing Grandsons: Robin and Jonathan Tucker (of T[...] and Matthew Bingham (of Tony), Charlie Bingham (of Cecilia), Bingham, Jr. (of Kim), Ole Hanson (of Ben). Missing Grea[...] Maggie), Nathan Bingham (of Ben). Missing Grea[...] Goddard (of Jonathan Goddard), and Mark Bin[...] Alexandra)

GRANDSONS: (Standing, Left to Right, In Ore[...] Richard, Jeremy and Alexander Tucker (of [...] John), Jonathan Goddard (of Cecilia), Dav[...]

Goddard (of Cecilia), Jerry Bingham (of [...] Ben), Sam Endicott, with bass guitar[...] Simon Bingham (of Ben), Chester [...] Bingham (of John), Joey Hanson (of [...] GREAT GRANDSONS: (Squating In [...] Elias Tucker (of Richard III), W[...] Bingham (of John, Jr.)

Most of Rose and Harry's twenty-nine grandchildren at the "Bingham Camp," Salem, Connecticut, circa 1996. Grandsons on the left; granddaughters on the right.

THE ROSE AND HIRAM BINGHAM GRANDDAUGHTERS!

(Missing Maia Rose Bingham!)

Left to Right: Racey (of John), Candor (of Ben), Eloise Godd[...] Celia), Olivia (of Tony), Tiffany (of David), Alexandra (of [...] Nan (of David).

Rose and all eleven children home for Thanksgiving, 1955. Left to right, Bill, Rose, Tony, Tiffany, Thomas, John, David, Robert Kim, Cecilia, Abigail, Margaret, Benjamin.

The Family

Rose Bingham (sixth from right in back row) with children, grandchildren, nieces, nephews at the beach in Waterford, Connecticut, circa 1975.

Rose and Harry with their children, Salem, Connecticut, circa 1953.

Harry Bingham playing the cello.

Harry Bingham's children proudly promote his newly invented "Florball" racquets, circa 1949.

SPORTATRON®

or any equivalent compact Cage-Court.

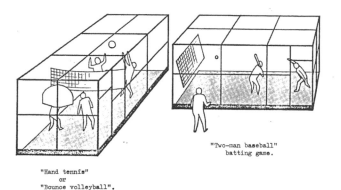

"Two-man baseball"
batting game.

"Hand tennis"
or
"Bounce volleyball".

Cage-court basketba
(six games).

Construction details and Rules for Games may be obtained from
Hiram Bingham → *INVENTOR*
(+CONSULTANT)
Salem, Connecticut 06415

Sportatron, a patented invention of Harry Bingham.

"golf" and the rebound net for batting and squash) and tinkered with many models of his enclosed fresh air minigym, the Sportatron.

His curious mind was directed both to the natural world and to the spiritual world that stands behind all existence.

I remember as a ten-year-old being allowed to sit up with him in our parlor in Buenos Aires with interesting visitors. He encouraged his children . . . to participate in his conversations with visitors in order to learn about life and be accustomed to stretching their minds. . . .

He had inspired ideas of minigym highways where one could stop for exercise and fun, or cities with roofs and miniparks alive with multiple Sportatrons. But the demand was not there for enclosed recreation that needed supervision to keep the nets and equipment functioning.

He did not have the business skills or assistance to bring traction to his ideas. . . .

Dad's keen interest in new ideas covered a wide range of interests, from tennis techniques and bird songs, to new social ideas of associative economic cooperation, to pure science, such as the nature of gravity, to spiritual science. . . .

In his forty-two years of struggling on the arduous path of spiritual development through the faculty of thinking, he often shared his new "discoveries" enthusiastically with others, like scattering seeds of wisdom and letting them fall on fertile or stony ground, as in the Parable. . . . Of course his work with the Rescue Committee in Marseilles was his own free ethical morality at work.

My sister Abigail Endicott recalls how Bingham enjoyed making his children laugh and play, and how devoted he was to Rose:

Dad's words when he was approaching his eightieth birthday show well what molded his character and how much his own family meant to him. I believe this is why he couldn't bear to separate families when he was helping refugees, and why he felt such deep sorrow over those he couldn't help that he didn't want to talk about that terrible time.

He was such a wonderful, loving father! He always seemed to enjoy times when we needed him to help us get breakfast, or pick us up, or drive us somewhere. I loved sharing chores with him, like shoveling snow, milking our one family cow, mowing the lawn, or even hand washing the many dishes, because he was always figuring out the most efficient way to do things, and he taught me to "do everything with love." He made everything we did interesting and fun when we were together.

He believed spiritual health is directly related to physical health and recreation, so he spent many fun hours teaching us sports and other skills to enjoy: ice skating, tennis, touch football, baseball, horseback riding just in the fields, ballroom dancing, acrobatics, songs, creative painting and drawing, hiking to enjoy nature, star gazing, and hilarious Sportatron games. He would laugh with us, sometimes until tears rolled down our cheeks, when some awkward play or ball bouncing on someone's head reduced us all to giggles.

He had an infectious enthusiasm about learning. He wanted me to keep an open mind in discussions, but was passionate about the need to avoid wrong behavior.

The sense of deep, romantic love between him and our mother was a role model, which gave me faith in true love that helped me find it myself.

Bingham's nephew Stephen Bingham fondly recalls Harry's dedication to sports:

I think my favorite memories of Uncle Harry are his various athletic endeavors. When we were still at Salem School, your father was getting all of us enthused about "Florball" and all the other games that could be played in the "Sportatron." It never made sense to me why there weren't Sportatrons everywhere. Uncle Harry felt so strongly that all of you [his eleven children] should be good athletes! A contrast with my family when we were growing up. He was good at whatever sport he was playing, especially as I remember, tennis.

His love of art is revealed in this report from my aunt, June Bingham (Birge), who recalls Bingham's wedding present to

her and her husband, the late Congressman Jonathan "Jack" Bingham (D-NY)—one of Harry's brothers:

Harry and Rose sent Jack and me the most marvelous wedding present in September 1939. It was a check for $250 with the stipulation that it be spent within six months for a single object (no fair just plopping it into the carpet fund for our new apartment), or it would be withdrawn. This lit a fire under us, and we spent most Saturdays at Knoedler Gallery where a friend of Jack's, Coe Kerr, was working. He let us into their attic where lots of paintings for small prices could be found in piles. One day we came across an Utrillo watercolor with gouache which we loved. It cost $500. So out from our carpet fund came another $250 to match Harry's and Rose's, and the painting still hangs in the living room. When I die, it will go to the Lehman College Art Gallery.

Harry Seemed Haunted by Those He Could Not Save

My cousin Lucretia Bingham, a freelance writer, notes that Bingham, beneath the surface, most likely remained haunted by those he could not save in the lengthy lines of refugees at Marseilles:

I believe the thought of those he hadn't saved during those World War years haunted him more than the comfort of those he did save. None of us can truly face the horror of the Holocaust without having lived through it ourselves. The most we can do is try to honor the souls of those who bravely tried, in the face of opposition, to do something actual to try and remedy and save those fleeing from persecution. . . .

With love and respect for the memory of Hiram Bingham, his niece,

Lucretia Bingham

This observation is akin to Bingham's "endless despair about his powerlessness" to save other refugees from the Holocaust, noted by Marta Feuchtwanger in her memoir regarding her refuge in 1940 at Bingham's villa with her husband Lion

Feuchtwanger (in the Postscript by Marta Feuchtwanger in 1987 edition to *The Devil in France*, originally published by Lion Feuchtwanger in 1941):

We felt safe for the moment since we were on the U.S. soil of the American Consulate, not knowing that the private villa of Consul Hiram Bingham did not enjoy that immunity. . . .

Lion, whom Bingham only permitted to leave the house after sundown to take a few steps, was concentrating on the third part of his Josephus novel and was unaware of the present and of his surroundings. Only Bingham was depressed, frequently filled with an endless despair about his powerlessness. The State Department had prohibited him from issuing the necessary visas to the people who were besieging the Consulate. I myself remember that after my escape from the camp at Gurs, I saw lines of people, several blocks long, young and old and very old who stood all day in the hot sun. They told me that it was like that every day.

No doubt, Bingham longed to forget the despair he felt during the dark days of the Holocaust. He succeeded in hiding his World War II experiences from his children, like the other diplomatic rescuers, whose heroic deeds have only recently come to light through the world-traveling "Visas for Life" exhibit.

Bingham's son John recalls how Rose vigorously protected Bingham's reputation as a law-abiding official, especially in front of his children. She would never let the children hear that their father might have broken—or stretched—the law while serving in the diplomatic corps:

I remember Dad frequently spinning his magical, pre-war "occupation" stories into what often bordered on exciting, "unconventional" territory, including the many times he told us, and sometimes our friends and dinner guests, about Lion Feuchtwanger's extraction from the swimming hole near the detention camp. It was clearly questionable behavior for diplomats to engage in, but he was usually covering his tracks with carefully chosen words, protecting either others or himself.

Eventually Mother, listening to his every word as her eyes and fork calmly chased peas around her plate, would, more loudly as the years progressed and little ears multiplied, rather abruptly and predictably (it was part of the drama

I sought) interject at just the pinnacle moment, "Harry!?"

He would always catch himself up short, as if it were planned that way. And in the boulder-heavy silence she had commanded, she would add her mantra, "Children, your father always acted within the law." And Dad, with a grinning glance through gold-rimmed spheres at his plate, would fork up a little bite of magnified Spam, chew quickly, and, ignoring our (my!) pleas for more details, resume his spinning with remnants of some lesser incident of that life in France in those heady days before war was declared, or with "Who would like to go riding with me tomorrow?"

Dad's frequent precipitous descent, through tales of his predilections to dissent from consular edicts, was always with Mother in the room, at his side as it were, perhaps for his safety, to rein him in and save him from his own certain despair in the remembering, despair that seemed so often very near the surface. He never talked of these things in private, without Mother in earshot, at least not to me. Unchecked, he might have revealed too much and slid grimly, out of control into that certain slough of despond, of lives abandoned, of anger at his government and nation, of impotence in not having done more than he did and not rising up more fiercely when restrained and removed by his government.

That's the mood, with uncertainty of the facts, that I remember Mother and Dad, as a team, enabling. It wasn't important who did what to whom when. They, "Harry's friends," were all in complicity in the game of saving lives, equally responsible, and in the habit of protecting each other, with uncertain facts, from the malice of present and future critics and enemies.

And Mother, the referee, strictly observed and kept Dad's play within the instructive boundaries of the field of rectitude. . . . That's how I saw it.

Harry Bingham's Notes on Approaching Eighty

On May 26 and June 25, 1983, as Bingham approached his eightieth birthday (July 17), he looked back on his life, highlighting the things he most wanted to remember. These handwritten words show how he was perceived by others and reveal his own motivations and joys. The following notes were found among his personal papers after his death in Mumford House.

"80"

Notes by Harry Bingham

May 16, 1983

In Celebration of my Gratitude for all the Wonderful Experiences of the Gift of Life and Love including the Experience Today of Completing Eight Full Decades of Life on This Extraordinary Planet Earth. As I approach my birthday I am thinking over as many of my memories as I can which have made these years so rich and wonderful. There is no question that I have been blessed— blessed with family and friends—my best friends are my family—at the center of which now is my adorable darling marvelous wife—

Blessed in the past with extraordinarily fine

parents—both Father and Mother great souls—
who did so much to start us off right in a confused
world at a critical time in history.

Speaking of blessings I must mention the
Beatitudes [Matthew 5:3-11] which I think we had
to learn by heart in Sacred Studies during my
First-Form year at Groton. They made a tremen-
dous impression which I've never forgotten.

Of all Christian teachings they were my favor-
ites—and just as rich in meaning as the two Com-
mandments to love God and neighbor and the Lord's
Prayer as the foundation of all Christian ethics.

The great services in Battell Chapel in our
early days in New Haven and the sermons at
Groton of the Rector [Endicott Peabody] and Mr.
Billings did a lot to stimulate my belief in the
importance of Christianity and helped to satisfy
my hunger and thirst for righteousness.—

"Blessed are they who hunger and thirst after
righteousness for they shall be filled."

Of course I didn't understand exactly what
this meant and I still don't—but in my days at

Groton I was teased unmercifully for being "Righteous." Why I was called "Righteous" I never could understand because I didn't think of myself as self-righteous at all. But it must have been partly because I judged others for not being perfect and for not believing as strongly as I did in Christian principles.

Life was not at all completely pleasant for me in those days at Groton. But I never blamed the School. I thought my lack of popularity was mostly my own fault but I didn't understand it until I learned much later in life during our years in Argentina about Dale Carnegie's ideas about how to make friends and influence people. That made life much easier.

June 25, 1983

The school motto at Groton was "Cui servire est regnare." ("Whom to serve is to rule.") The emphasis was on service and service to mankind and leadership—leadership in the church, in the government or in one of the professions. I thought of becoming a doctor and saw my first operation at Groton.

At Yale I started to study science—math was my best subject, but when I asked what light, electricity, and gravity were—I was told that nobody really knew—"God knows!" they said—so I started to take an interest in religion, and my favorite course was by a professor of Philosophy, Prof. Bennett, who gave a course in Ethics. One of our textbooks was *The Philosophy of Loyalty* by Royce. Love is important—of first importance—but it can't exist without loyalty.

While still at Groton, I learned that religion by one definition was "giving the best that you have to the best that you know."

The best I knew were the beatitudes—especially the one about hungering and thirsting for righteousness. I sought the best church but couldn't find one that I was sure was the best.

When I kept asking questions and not getting clear answers, I kept seeking. . . .

(Story—girl to boy who was proposing to her— "Why be so serious?" —To which he replied "Who's serious?")

Gravestone of Hiram Bingham IV and Rose Lawton Morrison Bingham in Salem, Connecticut, which simply reads: "Beloved parents of eleven children."

Anyway, I loved serious philosophical conversations and luckily got started into the Foreign
Service—diplomacy, where I was thrilled at the
first-hand view of the world.

Four wonderful years in the Far East, eight in
Europe, and four in South America—during which
I met and married the best possible mother for
my children and companion for myself. Far more
wonderful than I had dreamed of ever finding!

Chapter 7

State Department Finally Recognizes Harry Bingham's "Constructive Dissent"

Secretary of State Colin Powell was the first Secretary of State publicly to praise Bingham's actions in Marseilles. In a speech during the American Foreign Service Association awards ceremony at the State Department on June 27, 2002, Powell posthumously presented the "Constructive Dissent" award to Bingham's children and grandchildren, saying:

This proud tradition of service has deep roots in American history and in the Foreign Service. Later in today's ceremony, we'll be honoring the memory of Harry Bingham IV, a U.S. Vice Consul in Marseilles who risked his life and his career, put it on the line, to help over 2,500 Jews and others who were on Nazi death lists to leave France for America in 1940 and 1941. I am especially, especially honored and pleased to welcome here today in the audience two people who owe their lives to Harry Bingham's "visas of freedom," two people who got out because Harry was prepared to take that risk to career to do that which he knew was right.

The *Washington Post* reported on June 28, 2002:

The special constructive dissent award that went posthumously to Hiram Bingham IV, who defied State Department policy during World War II by surreptitiously issuing . . . visas to Jews desperate to flee Nazism . . . Powell called Bingham a diplomat "who risked his life and his career" to do the right thing. Thomas Pickering, a seven-time ambassador who received an award yesterday for contributions to U.S. diplomacy, also paid homage to Bingham's "creative integrity."

Bingham was one of the "Righteous and Honorable Diplomats" featured in the world-traveling "Visas for Life" exhibitions that opened in Washington, D.C., in October 2003. Secretary Powell greeted families of the other diplomats as well. (The title "Righteous and Honorable Diplomats" denotes those diplomats who have already been awarded Yad Vashem's "Righteous Among the Nations" status, as well as others, like Bingham, who have been nominated for it but who have not received it.)

One who was rescued by Bingham, Rabbi Joseph Schachter, responded to my stamp-drive website and sent me a poignant e-mail message. He even attached copies of the visas Bingham had issued to his family of six. I was thrilled to see my father's familiar signatures on these documents and also on "affidavits in lieu of passports" that Bingham had provided to the Schachters sixty-two years before. Rabbi Schachter e-mailed on April 2003:

I and my entire immediate family (six persons in all) had received the life-saving visas, dated Feb. 7, 1941. . . .

My sister, who has the originals, hastened to let all those to whom I had forwarded the news story that it was more than just a supposition that he [Bingham] had issued the visas—but that she had the original documents. . . . I was just ten years old at the time and do not remember any details other than a sense of relief that we were going to be able to escape the impending disaster, having already had three "brushes" with the Gestapo: in Vienna in 1938 from which we fled to Belgium, and from Antwerp which we fled in May 1940, and in the Occupied portion of France from which we managed to make our way south. Our parents—Salomon and Gitta Schachter, accompanied by four children aged 17, 10, 8, and 7—were able to embark on Feb. 17 by way of the Antilles and reach U.S. territory, the Virgin Islands in March. . . .

Our parents are gone now, but there are quite a number of grandchildren and great-grandchildren scattered in many parts of the United States and Canada, and some of us now reside in Israel. We have as a result of the news story passed on the very aspect of their existence as having been dramatically affected by the actions of Hiram Bingham IV. . . .

To paraphrase my mother's saying: "When he reaches Paradise, he will find a multitude of greeters welcoming him and thanking him!" If we can be of any help in the project for a commemorative stamp, I'd be delighted to enlist the entire family and friends.

—Rabbi Joseph Schacter

In January 2000, survivor Lilian Stuart Smith wrote a letter to the editor of the *Foreign Service Journal* in support of the Bingham stamp:

Hiram Bingham . . . did not hesitate to issue visas for our entire family. I learned later that he helped many people who were in danger from the Germans. His courage and generosity cost him much. The Germans complained of his activities to the Vichy government, who then complained to Washington.

Centennial Celebration

Survivor Ralph M. Hockley wrote a message on what would have been Bingham's one-hundredth birthday (July 17, 2003):

Dear Kim Bingham,

From the Pacific Northwest where my wife and I are traveling, please receive our sincere wishes on the occasion of your father's 100th Birthday. Please relay to your family on this important occasion of celebration of your father's life, my family's eternal thanks for what Hiram Bingham did in 1940-1941. I have just explained to my sister's

The Awards

On behalf of the American Foreign Service Association (AFSA), Secretary of State Colin Powell presented a posthumous "Constructive Dissent" award to Harry Bingham's children at a State Department ceremony on June 27, 2002. Left to right, David, Benjamin, AFSA President John Naland (back), Tony, Secretary of State Colin Powell, Abigail Endicott, John (back), Maia (granddaughter), Robert Kim, Bill.

Secretary of State Colin Powell greets Bingham's daughter Abigail and son Robert Kim Bingham at a State Department "Visas for Life" ceremony in October 2003.

Secretary of State Colin Powell addresses the "Visas for Life" diplomatic families, October 2003.

Author Robert Kim Bingham holds Foreign Service Journal featuring his father, Hiram Bingham IV.

nineteen-year-old grandson that without your father, he probably would never have been born. What more can I say?

Sincere greetings from Ralph M. Hockley and sister Marianne Pennekamp

Survivor Pierre Shostal wrote in July 2003:

Thanks so much for sending such eloquent testimonies of your Dad's heroism on the occasion of his 100th birthday. As you well know, I am one of the many who would not be on this earth if he had not helped my family. I think about him often, and bless his name. I also wanted to let you know that my father passed away on July 3, at the age of 95. He had a peaceful end, and we had some very good conversations in his last months. I am thankful to you and your family also for giving him the opportunity to recall the circumstances in which we received our visa in Marseilles. With warm wishes,

Pierre Shostal

I received letters from other well-wishers for Bingham's hundredth birthday anniversary on July 17, 2003. The Right Reverend Jeffery Rowthorn, a retired Episcopal suffragan bishop of Connecticut and former bishop of the Episcopal Church in Europe, wrote on that date:

[I wish] to express my deep admiration for the courage and faith which your father showed when serving in Marseilles during the darkest days of the Second World War. On this hundredth anniversary of his birth, I rejoice that an Episcopalian with ties to Salem offered so bold a witness when others stood by and did nothing. You know at first hand from the families involved how his actions gave life and hope back to countless persecuted Jews.

It has been my privilege to preach about your remarkable father/father-in-law, and one of these days I would like to see him included in the Calendar of the Episcopal Church as testimony to what faithfulness in daily life can mean, and what one person can achieve on behalf of others. Praise God on this special day!

Jeffery

Eric Saul, Director of "Visas for Life" at the Simon Wiesenthal Center, wrote:

Bingham's view of refugees from his Marseilles consulate office window, circa 1940.

Subject: Happy 100th Birthday Harry!

From: Eric Saul, Simon Wiesenthal Center

Dear Bingham Family,

I'd like to take this opportunity to wish the
family of Hiram "Harry" Bingham IV a wonderful
centennial birthday celebration. Your father,
grandfather, uncle, and friend was a great and
courageous man. I would like to reflect on the
heroic spirit of the late Harry Bingham on the

centennial of his birth, July 17, 1903. To many Jews and non-Jews, Harry Bingham was a life-saver. The Jewish Talmud, which is the commentary on the five books of Moses, has a phrase, "If you save the life of even one person, it is as if you had saved the entire world." This phrase meant that saving the life of the person in fact saved every person in succeeding generations until the end of time. Your father, serving as the Vice-Consul in charge of visas in Marseilles, 1940-41, was responsible for issuing visas to hundreds of Jewish refugees and others fleeing the Nazis. At least three generations have passed since your father's actions in Marseilles. We can only begin to imagine how many lives he has touched, and how many people can claim their rescue by your father's actions. We can also only begin to imagine the accomplishments of these individuals and their descendants to make our world a better place.

The Talmud also teaches that it is the highest nobility for a person to maintain his goodness in evil times. There is a phrase that "just doing your job at times is just not doing your job." Your father, by breaking the rules of an indifferent American government, was following his higher conscience. The Talmud further states that the righteous person is guaranteed a place of honor in the world to come. . . .

I first became aware of Hiram Bingham IV in 1996 from the curators of the Varian Fry exhibit at the U.S. Holocaust Memorial Museum in Washington, D.C. They told me that I should include your father in the Visas for Life exhibit about diplomats who rescued Jews and other refugees during the war. . . . On behalf of the Visas for Life families, I would like to wish your family a happy commemorative centennial celebration of your father.

Shalom, Eric

Other Recognitions

Bingham received other memorable posthumous tributes.

I have already mentioned that in 1993 the U.S. Holocaust Memorial Museum in Washington, D.C., sent Rose and Harry

Bingham an invitation to attend a remarkable outdoor tribute to World War II rescuers in the Arlington National Cemetery Amphitheater. Because Harry Bingham had already died, and it was too long a distance for my mother to travel, she forwarded the invitations to my sister Abigail and me, who lived in the Washington, D.C., area at the time. My mother asked us to attend on her and my late father's behalf. It was a spectacular event, with military bands playing and flags gleaming from countries of several Allies in World War II.

This celebration was our first clue that our father might be recognized outside the family, at least by the U.S. Holocaust Museum, as a World War II rescuer, and we were very proud of him.

Five years later, in April 1998, the Yad Vashem Museum in Jerusalem sponsored the "Visas for Life" exhibit in honor of eleven World War II diplomats who had saved lives, including Bingham—the only American diplomat honored at that time. Three of Harry's sons were invited to tour Israel and attend the exhibit.

In 1999, the Holocaust Memorial Committee of New Bedford, Massachusetts, sponsored a "Visas for Life" exhibit, which also included Bingham. My brother Dr. David Bingham was a guest speaker.

On April 3, 2000, U.N. Secretary General Kofi Annan gave a keynote address at the opening of the "Visas for Life" exhibit at the United Nations in New York, which again included Bingham. The Secretary General praised the World War II diplomats who had saved lives from the Holocaust:

Some famous, others known to just a few, they

make up a gallery of courageous individuals
who, in the face of an inhuman force that was
destroying lives and societies alike, took enor-
mous personal risks to rescue Jews and others
facing persecution and peril. They were true
heroes; indeed, they were among the foremost
human rights defenders of their day.

On October 18, 2001, Connecticut Secretary of the State
Susan Bysiewicz dedicated the official state manual ("blue
book") to Bingham. In her speech, given at a dedication ceremony conducted at Yale's Peabody Museum, she said:

It is then, with great pride and admiration, that I
dedicate the 2001 edition of the Connecticut State
Register and Manual to Hiram Bingham IV, truly a
righteous and honorable man.

At the time of Bingham's "Constructive Dissent" award ceremony at the State Department in June 2002, he was featured in a
long cover-story article in the *Foreign Service Journal* (June, 2002).

On April 17, 2004, on the campus of the Catholic University
of America, just before the start of a dramatic concert entitled
"Defiant Requiem—Verdi at Terezin," the Very Reverend David
M. O'Connell, president of the university, gave a speech about
Bingham and posthumously awarded him the Catholic University
of America's President's Medal. The medal was accepted by
Harry's eighth child, Abigail. President O'Connell said:

Hiram Bingham IV chose principle over expediency and humanity over political calculation. He displayed courage in defiance of evil. For these reasons, the Catholic University of America is proud to confer posthumously upon him its highest honor, the President's Medal.

Around 1999, major newspapers also began reporting about Bingham as an "unsung hero." The *New York Times* wrote:

"Bingham is remarkable because he was willing to respond to orders from the State Department—orders that went against his grain—appropriately," said Susan Morgenstein, consultant to the United States Holocaust Memorial Museum. Ms. Morgenstein is a consultant who was hired by the Holocaust Museum to be curator for the Fry exhibition.

"In the south of France, Mr. Bingham responded in his own humane and righteous way for the good of our nation perhaps at a time when his superiors were giving orders that went against that good land we should be," she said. "He can be credited for going with his instincts for good, and against what he knew was ill-intentioned."

...he jeopardized

Harry Bingham portrait, circa 1935.

both his career and his life

—Ilene Pachman

(Maura Casey, "A Diplomat's Battle to Save Jews Emerges," Connecticut Edition of *New York Times*, July 11, 1999.)

The *Washington Post* reported:

Harry Bingham . . . became an extraordinary unsung hero of the American diplomatic corps. Bingham jeopardized both his career and his life in the early years of World War II to help rescue Jews and anti-Nazi activists while he was stationed in Marseilles, France. For this work in the years 1939–41, he was reassigned . . . and held back professionally through the rest of his career.

(Ilene Pachman, Op/Ed, July 28, 2001.)

Chapter 8

WELCOME TO JERUSALEM

ישראל מקדמת בברכה
דיפלומטים שפעלו להצלת יהודים
נערך בשיתוף עם מרכז שמעון

...AEL WELCOMES THE
...IPLOMATS WHO SAV...
FROM THE HOLOC...

אכסניות נוער בישראל
...ת משתתפ...מצ...חיים

Story of the Stamp Drive and the Unveiling of the Hiram Bingham IV Stamp

My inspiration for the Harry Bingham stamp drive arose during a special tour of Israel in 1998.

We children of World War II "Righteous and Honorable Diplomats" were invited by the Simon Wiesenthal Center, Los Angeles, to tour Israel during Israel's Fiftieth Anniversary celebrations in April 1998, when the Yad Vashem museum opened the "Visas for Life" exhibit in honor of the eleven diplomats, including Harry Bingham, who collectively rescued an estimated 200,000 refugees from the Holocaust.

This tour was a very moving experience. At various venues around Israel, we listened to survivors' gripping stories of escapes from the Holocaust, and their constant expressions of gratitude to our diplomatic fathers who had saved many lives.

We were invited to the unveiling of a new Israeli stamp series honoring four of the "Righteous and Honorable Diplomats" (my father was not among them). Afterwards, I had a conversation with one of the diplomat's children who, apparently speaking from experience, said how difficult it is to get any government to issue a stamp.

That remark started me thinking that this would be a good challenge for me to undertake. While recalling the many joyous hours together with my father collecting stamps, I did not think this modest man would protest too loudly, were he alive. When we returned from Israel in May, the first thing I did was to write an article about our tour of Israel for the *New London Day*, which appeared on May 24, 1998. I mentioned the poignant stories of survivors of the Holocaust that I heard on the tour—and how grateful they still are to diplomats who saved them. My emotion was contagious, I assume, as even U.S. Senator Joseph I. Lieberman wrote that he was moved to tears by my piece. I still have his letter of June 23, 1998, in which he stated:

Your article in the *New London Day* about your family's trip to Israel was very moving. It literally brought tears to my eyes. Your father was a righteous hero, and I am so pleased his heroism is finally receiving the attention and gratitude it deserves.

Next, I learned that to receive the honor of a stamp, U.S. Postal Service rules required that the honoree be a U.S. citizen, and be deceased at least ten years. Since both official criteria were satisfied, I sent a lengthy petition to the Postmaster General, urging that a Harry Bingham IV stamp be issued, listing a number of reasons. I stressed that Bingham was a U.S. government servant who deserved recognition for doing the right thing, particularly after Swedish diplomat Raoul Wallenberg, who was made an honorary citizen, received recognition on a U.S. stamp in 1997.

Through the Southern New England Telephone Company, I created a stamp-drive website for Harry Bingham and drafted and posted different petition forms for lawmakers and private citizens to sign and return to me— for forwarding to the Postmaster General (see website directory, petition forms, and proposed legislative resolutions at http://pages.cthome.net/WWIIHERO/). I downloaded about 120 pages of material onto the website, including a draft "Joint Resolution" for the Congress to pass, and created a website directory.

I also contacted many politicians' offices by phone and e-mail, and made visits to Congress, distributing supporting documents about Harry Bingham to U.S. Senators and Representatives. Everyone of those I contacted—perhaps twenty-five lawmakers or their aides—were favorably disposed to sign petitions to either the Postmaster General or Citizens' Stamp Advisory Committee (the committee that makes stamp recommendations to the Postmaster General).

The favorable bipartisan responses I received on Capitol Hill bolstered my enthusiasm. I came back to Connecticut ready to make frequent visits to photocopy outlets, putting together many

Families of diplomats visiting Israel (left to right): John Paul Abranches, son of Portuguese diplomat Aristides de Sousa Mendes; Valerie Komor, daughter of Hungarian diplomat Paul Komor; Robert Kim Bingham, son of American diplomat Harry Bingham; Mrs. Chiune Sugihara, widow of Japanese diplomat Chiune Sugihara; Manli Ho, daughter of Chinese diplomat Dr. Feng Shan Ho, April 1998. In the background, large signs welcome the diplomatic families.

The Israel Tour

Part of "Harry's Wall" at Yad Vashem Museum,
Jerusalem, circa 1998.

VISAS FOR LIFE:
THE RIGHTEOUS DIPLOMATS
MISSION TO ISRAEL
IN COOPERATION WITH THE SIMON WIESENTHAL CENTER

37-707-00

Sign on the "Visas for Life" tour bus in Israel.

Above: In April 1998, three sons of Harry Bingham planted a tree in the Sugihara Forest.

Left: Pine tree planted in honor of Hiram Bingham IV.

more such packages about Harry, and writing open letters and press releases, which I mailed to various celebrities and organizations. The e-mail and website were effective new tools for contacting many people simultaneously and keeping them abreast of developments during the campaign, including news and letters received, and recent recognitions given to Bingham. I heard from just one irate naysayer who not only opposed honoring Harry, but was also bent on defaming "Visas for Life," Yad Vashem, and even a famous Holocaust survivor—until he was finally repudiated by the Jewish community.

I contacted the national headquarters of different religious organizations, corporate executives, Hollywood stars, talk-show hosts, TV and radio network news organizations, and heads of non-profit associations and societies. The American Jewish Committee, in particular, provided strong early support for the HBIV stamp, and later sponsored a "Visas for Life" program at their annual convention in Washington, D.C., that included Bingham among the honorees.

The Connecticut delegation of U.S. Senators and U.S. Representatives was most encouraging and signed letters of support to the Postmaster General, as did, eventually, forty U.S. Senators and thirty-nine U.S. Representatives. Connecticut Senators Christopher Dodd and Joseph Lieberman wrote several letters to the Postmaster General between 1999 and 2005.

Incredibly, two state representatives from Connecticut—former State Representative Rob Simmons and State Representative Linda Orange—managed to obtain the unanimous support of the entire Connecticut legislature. All 151 state representatives and 36 state senators affixed their signatures to the HBIV stamp proposal. In addition, the governor declared "Hiram Bingham IV Day" in Connecticut several years in a row.

Meanwhile, the stamp campaign became a front-page headline in the *Norwich Bulletin*. The *New London Day* and other regional and national newspapers also printed affirmative articles about the stamp drive. In addition, the United Nations' "Visas for Life" exhibit generated wide publicity. This exhibit continued to travel to museums and other venues around the world, generating more press. The Jewish Federation of Eastern Connecticut sponsored an exhibit at Connecticut College, New London. The History Channel came to Harry's home in Salem to film his family and his story for a program entitled "Diplomats for the Damned," which periodically airs on national television.

Writer Ilene Pachman of Pennsylvania, who had successfully campaigned for the Raoul Wallenberg stamp, wrote an article in the *Washington Post* entitled "Honor This Hero" (July 28, 2001), urging Secretary of State Colin Powell to support the HBIV stamp campaign :

I'd like to invite the secretary [Colin Powell] to join in an effort . . . to honor another American diplomat . . . Hiram Bingham IV.

[The] quest for approval of a commemorative stamp is an uphill journey. Each year the CSAC [Citizens' Stamp Advisory Committee] receives proposals for some 2,000 different subjects. From these, the committee recommends a limited

Robert Kim Bingham campaigned six years for Harry Bingham's stamp.

Binghams seek tangible honor for father's heroism

Sons seek postage stamp in name of man who saved Jews from Nazis

By ROBERT WESTERVELT
Day Staff Writer

Salem — The sons of Hiram Bingham IV hope to put a stamp of approval on the heroic diplomatic career of their late father.

Robert Kim Bingham and his brothers David and William knew only bits and pieces about the wartime past of their father. Hiram Bingham did not talk about his service as a diplomat in Europe shortly before World War II. They knew only that their father helped save some well-known painters, novelists and philosophers from Hitler's Nazi concentration camps.

Nearly 10 years after his death in 1988, the true heroism of their father became clear to his 11 adult children. They discovered an accumulation of "Harry" Bingham's diaries and documents in a linen closet in the Bingham family's 230-year-old homestead here.

For the past four years Robert Kim Bingham has been on a crusade of sorts. He's been trying to persuade the Citizens Stamp Advisory Committee, a national-level group that meets four times a year, to approve a postage stamp in honor of his father.

A postage stamp would top the list of awards and recognitions that Hiram Bingham has received since his death in 1988, the son said. Momentum has been building for his cause.

The American Foreign Service Officers' Association will honor the diplomat for his heroic service during the Holocaust by presenting the Bingham family with a special posthumous award at the association's annual awards ceremony in June. Additionally, the Foreign Service Journal, a publication of the American Foreign Service Association, will devote its June cover story to Bingham.

Bingham thinks a decision could

See **BINGHAM** *page* C4

SUZANNE OUELLETTE / The Day

■ *Robert Kim Bingham, surrounded by family photos, holds one of his parents, Hiram Bingham IV and Rose Morrison Bingham, at his Salem home Saturday.*

THE DAY, TUESDAY, MAY 28, 2002

Bingham family would like stamp to honor Dad

From **C1**

come as early as this fall on whether a Bingham stamp is to be included in the 2003 commemorative stamp lineup.

"His story could bring some joy to those that think about the horrors of the Holocaust," he said. "There are people that fight evil even in the worst of times, and my father was one of those people."

The papers found by the sons included reports on the concentration camps, maps of escape routes and notes on meetings of anti-Nazi conspirators. Phony documents and papers used by escapees to gain freedom, as well as black and white photos of prisoners in concentration camps, were among the papers.

Among those Bingham helped to safety were Russian surrealist artist Marc Chagall, German surrealist painter Max Ernst, French painter and writer André Masson, writers Victor Serge and Franz Werfel and Nobel Prize-winning biochemist Otto Meyerhof. Home movies of Chagall were part of the collection the Binghams found.

"The luminaries weren't the only ones. There were many people," Bingham said. "Even though what he did is considered heroic, he saw it

to visit the memorial and talk with survivors who say they owe their lives to Bingham.

A Swedish diplomat, Raoul Wallenberg, was made a U.S. citizen — a requirement to be depicted on a postage stamp — and honored with a stamp last year.

Bingham acted in direct opposition to official State Department orders that made immigration of refugees into the United States as difficult as possible, Robert Kim Bingham said. The diplomat avoided prosecution for violating official U.S. policy, partly because of contacts of his father, Hiram Bingham III, the former Connecticut governor and U.S. senator. Bingham was removed from his position in the spring of 1941 after his superiors in the State Department learned of his rescue activities. He was later transferred to Buenos Aires.

Frustrated by the government's unwillingness to investigate or stop the flow of war criminals and Nazi gold to Latin America, Bingham resigned and returned to the family home in Salem.

Robert Kim Bingham continues to seek support for the stamp by getting as many people as possible to write to the Postmaster General. He has a

■ *Hiram Bingham IV, the U.S.*
Bingham family photo

Newspaper clippings about the campaign for the Bingham stamp.

number to the postmaster general.

This column caught the eyes of influential people in the Washington, D.C., area, including senior government official Pierre Shostal, whose own family, he recalled, was saved by Harry Bingham. I understand Shostal persuaded the president of the American Foreign Service Association, John Naland, and its board of directors, to honor Harry for his "Constructive Dissent" during their annual awards ceremony in June 2002. This was a crowning event at which Colin Powell, as noted above, personally presented the posthumous "Constructive Dissent" award to Harry's children in behalf of the association.

During the period 1998 to 2005, I kept enlarging Harry's official stamp file in Washington, D.C., by forwarding petitions, press coverage of the U.N. exhibit, and other recognitions.

Visitors to the website, who inquired about how to support the stamp, were typically e-mailed the address of the Citizens' Stamp Advisory Committee, a crucial committee of the U.S. Postal Service, and encouraged to write a letter of support to that committee. Each year, the U.S. Postal Service politely informed me that the HBIV stamp proposal "remain[ed] under consideration."

In November 2004, I received a stunning confidential telephone call from a U.S. Postal Service program manager in the "stamp development" division, Washington, D.C., indicating that Harry would be recognized on his own commemorative stamp in a series of six "Distinguished American Diplomats," to be issued in 2006. After catching my breath, and further discussion, I gave the postal official the names and addresses of the four trustees of Harry's estate, including me, who could sign a confidential agreement with the U.S. Postal Service, regarding publication rights and the stamp design, and assure that the matter remained confidential until the public announcement, made at the end of 2005.

On December 1, 2004, I again was exhilarated when the U.S. Postal Service sent me the official hard-copy proofs of Harry's 37-cent commemorative stamp design for 2006 (it actually came out as a 39-cent stamp in 2006; the price of stamps went up). I circulated the design to the trustees, who promptly approved it.

I remain indebted to the loyal supporters of the HBIV stamp drive who devoted their time and effort to this remarkable journey.

Unveiling the Hiram Bingham IV Stamp

Why did the U.S. Postal Service decide to issue a stamp for Harry? Probably the stamp drive would not have succeeded had broad bipartisan support been lacking.

Not to be discounted is the energetic support of Holocaust survivors Lilian Stuart Smith, Rabbi Joseph Schachter, Ralph Hockley, and Pierre Shostal, whose poignant stories made their way into Harry Bingham's official file in Washington.

Secretary Colin Powell's public recognition of Harry Bingham's "Constructive Dissent" and the American Foreign Service Association backing were also key.

On November 30, 2005, the Hiram Bingham IV stamp was publicly unveiled by the U.S. Postal Service, as part of a 2006 commemorative stamp series of six "Distinguished American Diplomats."

On May 30, 2006 (the first day of issue), CBS News correspondent Wyatt Andrews interviewed Elly Sherman (the eighty-year-old survivor saved by Bingham) and me for the nationally televised CBS Evening News.

In front of millions of viewers, Wyatt Andrews called Bingham an "American hero [who] quietly did the right thing." Wyatt Andrews also reported:

Bingham said little about what he had done, and his own family did not realize the scope of things until [some years] after his death. Bingham's heroism was recognized posthumously in 2002, and on Tuesday [May 30, 2006], a dream came true for his children as the U.S. Postal Service unveiled a stamp in Bingham's honor.

Elly Sherman, who was lined up with her family and other Jews outside the U.S. Consulate in Marseilles, where they were saved by Bingham, doesn't need a stamp to jog her memory.

"My mother kept this document," said Sherman, pointing to the long-ago paperwork [signed by Bingham] that allowed her family to flee as the Nazis marched forward into France.

"Sherman's family," Wyatt Andrews also said, "at the time the visas were issued had already received an order to report to a concentration camp within two days."

The Harry Bingham stamp.

The six "Distinguished American Diplomats."

By learning about Hiram Bingham IV, I hope that we as a society can further the cause of making this world a more humane and loving place. Having this hope is what my father's life is all about. His favorite motto, "Give the best that you have to the best that you know," informed his acts of courage and compassion during the bleak days of the Holocaust. Instead of saving souls like his missionary ancestors, the best that he knew was to stand up to evil by saving lives.

I can think of no better epitaph or memorial to my father than the immortal words of the poet of Ecclesiasticus:

But these were godly men, whose righteous deeds have not been forgotten. . . . Their bodies are buried in peace, but their name lives on generation after generation.

Timeline in France During World War II

January 30, 1933 Adolf Hitler appointed Chancellor of Germany.

March 22, 1933 Dachau concentration camp opens.

April 1, 1933 German boycott of Jewish shops and businesses. . . .

September 15, 1935 "Nuremberg Laws": anti-Jewish racial laws enacted; Jews no longer considered German citizens.

March 7, 1936 Germans march into the Rhineland, previously demilitarized by the Versailles Treaty.

March 14, 1938 Cheering crowds greet Hitler as he parades triumphantly through Vienna.

October 10, 1938 Hitler gives personal instructions to "act for the deportation of 27,000 Viennese Jews of Czech nationality."

October 28, 1938 In Austria, thousands of Jews who are Polish nationals are deported into the no-man's-land on the German-Polish border.

November 9-10, 1938 *Kristallnacht* (Night of Broken Glass): an anti-Jewish pogrom in Germany, Austria, and the Sudetenland; 200 synagogues are destroyed, cemeteries desecrated, 7,500 Jewish shops looted, and nearly 100 Jews murdered. Many Jews commit suicide in the following weeks and months; 30,000 German, Austrian, and Sudeten Jews are sent to concentration camps of Dachau, Buchenwald, and Sachsenhausen. Between 1938 and 1939, more than 1,000 Jews are murdered in these camps.

December 6, 1938 France and Germany sign nonaggression pact.

January 10, 1939 Hitler announces to the German Reichstag [Parliament] that a world war will result in "the annihilation of the Jewish race in Europe."

January 21, 1939 The French government opens first concentration camp for foreigners and Jewish refugees in the district of Mende.

September 1, 1939 Germany invades Poland. Beginning of World War II. . . . The French government enacts anti-Jewish measures against the Jews in Paris. There are between 300,000 and 330,000 Jews living in France; 200,000 live in Paris. This is less than one percent of the total population in France, which is 43 million. Three thousand German and Austrian Jews are interned in French camps as "undesirable aliens." The French government arrests German and Austrian nationals who have landed in French ports but who are bound for the Western Hemisphere. Most of these are Jews fleeing the Nazis. Most are interned in Les Milles detention camp. By the outbreak of war, nearly 70 percent or 185,246 Jews in Austria have emigrated. Many go to southern France.

Fall 1939 The French government opens numerous concentration camps throughout France to house the influx of refugees entering the country. Eventually, they become deportation centers to the Nazi death camps.

October 1, 1939 By this date, the Marseilles police arrest more than 13,000 Germans and Austrians, most of whom are Jews.

1940 French Premier Edouard Daladier resigns. He is succeeded by Paul Reynaud. Reynaud appoints World War I French hero Marshal Pétain as the Vichy premier.

April 9, 1940 Germany invades Denmark and Norway.

May 10, 1940 Germany invades France, the Netherlands, Belgium, and Luxembourg; and 136 German divisions participate in the invasion. Germans enforce anti-Jewish measures in each area. Soon, four million refugees are fleeing the onslaught of the Nazis.

June 11, 1940 General Weygood declares that the battle of France is lost and advises the French government to maintain order and avoid chaos of war. A million French soldiers are taken prisoner by the German armed forces. French government evacuates Paris.

June 14, 1940 Paris falls, and the French government is transferred to Bordeaux. More than one million refugees pour into the south of France, more than 195,000 of whom are Jews.

June 16, 1940 French Vichy government is established under World War I hero Marshal Philippe Pétain. Pétain becomes head of the French cabinet. Pétain asks for an armistice eight days before the fighting ceases.

June 22, 1940 France surrenders, and the French sign an armistice with Germany. The French armed forces are to be disarmed. Three-fifths of France is surrendered to German control. ✛ In Article 19 of the French armistice with Germany, the French agree to "surrender on demand all Germans named by the German government in France." ✛ Approximately 350,000 Jews reside in France at the time of the German invasion. They constitute less than one percent of the total population of France, which is 45 million. 150,000 Jews are French native-born. About 50,000 are recent refugees from Germany, Austria, Czechoslovakia, Hungary, and Romania. 50,000 are from the invaded countries of Belgium, Holland, and Luxembourg. An undetermined number of Eastern European, mostly Polish, Jews has entered the country after the German invasion of Poland. ✛ France becomes the largest population center for Jews in Western Europe. More than half of the Jews in France are in the south. Eventually, one-third of the Jewish refugees in the south return to Paris. ✛ Austrian and German Jews in France who are interned at Rieucros concentration camp are eventually sent south to camps in Vichy.

June 1940 Marshal Pétain is installed as head of state with Pierre Laval his Vice President of the Council of Ministers. Pétain is granted executive powers under the armistice agreement, and the French National Assembly is merely a "rubber stamp." Pétain abolishes the French constitution of 1875 and dismisses the French Senate and Chamber of Deputies. Pierre Laval is a Nazi collaborationist and puppet. ✛ Civil liberties in France are suspended. ✛ France is divided into two zones. The northern zone is administered by German military forces. The south, called the "Free Zone," is established in the resort town of Vichy. The Nazi military occupation forces control about two-thirds of France. ✤ Four million French, Belgian, Luxembourg, and other refugees have fled the German onslaught. ✤ France is forced to pay Germany 400 million francs a day as a war indemnity. ✤ The French begin to implement Nuremberg-style anti-Semitic laws imposed on all Jews in France. These laws and policies are initiated entirely by the Vichy government. These restrictive laws and decrees will eventually disenfranchise most foreign Jews in France.

Summer 1940 20,000 Jewish refugees from Germany, Austria, Holland, Belgium, and Luxembourg are interned in the 31 French camps in the southern unoccupied zone.

July 22, 1940 A French commission is set up to review French citizens who have been naturalized since 1927. It is set up with the intention of revoking the citizenship of citizens who are considered "undesirable." 15,000 people, including 6,000 Jews, have their citizenship revoked. ✤ Lion Feuchtwanger is staying at Hiram Bingham's house.

August 1940 American private citizen Varian Fry, appointed by the Emergency Rescue Committee (ERC), arrives in Marseilles, France. He is empowered to save artists, writers, composers, and other intellectuals who are on Hitler's arrest lists. Fry and his volunteers make contact with numerous rescue and relief agencies, including the Nîmes Committee. Fry and his volunteers also work with various foreign consular officials who issue him hundreds of legal and extra-legal visas and other documents to help Jews escape the Nazis. These diplomats include U.S. Vice Consul Hiram "Harry" Bingham, Mexican Consul General Gilberto Bosques, a Chinese diplomat, and Vladimir Vochoc, the Czech Consul in Marseilles. (Vladimir Vochoc is later arrested, but manages to escape to Lisbon.) Fry and his associates organize escape routes over the Pyrenees Mountains for refugees. Hans and Lisa Fittko are among his most able guides.

September 27, 1940 Rome-Berlin-Tokyo Axis alliance is signed. ✤ First anti-Semitic German law (*Verordnung*) is enacted in the occupied zone. It defines Jews by race. Under this law, the French Vichy government can arrest and send foreigners to the newly established labor camps. These camps are called Foreign Labor Battalion (GTE) camps. Prisoners are forced to work under severe conditions. Relief agencies in France protest the conditions in these camps.

October 3, 1940 French Vichy government enacts Statut des Juifs [Jewish Statute]. This law has constitutional authority. Under this law, Jews are defined as Jews not by religion, but by race. The law is signed by Pétain and Laval and eight members of the French government. It is a law that removes many Jewish civil rights. Jews are forbidden from holding government positions, military service, teaching, and other public positions. Unemployed Jews are now subject to internment. All Jews under the French and German laws must register with the French police. Jews must carry an ID card with the words "Juif" or "Juife" [Jew] in bold red letters.

October 4, 1940 The Vichy Law of October 4 authorizes French prefects to arrest and intern "foreigners of the Jewish race" in "special camps." ✤ Concentration camps in France are administered and staffed solely by Frenchmen. There are 31 camps established throughout France. Conditions are harsh and brutal. 50,000 Jews are interned in French camps in the north and south. 70 percent of those interned in the south are Jewish. Between 3,000 and 4,000 Jews die in these camps. The

camps are so inhumane that even Vichy officials complain. One official writes: "The internees' living conditions put the honor of France on the line." Even the German Red Cross is horrified by the conditions in the camps, which include starvation and death. News of the conditions in the camp is disseminated throughout the world.
✚ By the end of 1942, 42,000 internees in these camps will be transferred and killed in the death camps in Poland.

November 1940 40,000 Jews are deported from Lorraine to Lyons.

December 1940 Harry Bingham, U.S. vice consul in Marseilles, issues painter Marc Chagall a visa to leave France.

May 7, 1941 Fry writes in his diary: "Wednesday, May 7. Harry Bingham told me this morning that he has just received instructions to go to Lisbon. He is closing his house and packing his things. His going will be a great loss to the refugees, and may seriously cripple our work. He has been the one man at the Consulate who had always seemed to understand that his job now is not to apply the rules rigidly but to save lives whenever he could without actually violating United States law. Without his help, much of what we have done we could [not] have done. Especially since the opening of the Martinique route, he has worked very hard, minimizing formalities and always showing a sympathetic attitude towards candidates for immigration. His behavior has always been in sharp contrast to that of most other American Consuls in France. I hate to think what it is going to be like here after he has gone."

May 13-15, 1941 Pétain broadcasts pledge of cooperation with German occupying forces.
✚ Thousands of Polish Jews in Paris are rounded up pending deportation. They are deported to French concentration camps Pithiviers and Beaune-la-Rolande.
✚ SS Haputsturmführer (Captain) Theodore Dannecker meets with director of the German military rail system General Kohl. Kohl agrees to supply trains to deport between 10,000 and 20,000 French Jews in the next few months.

June 2, 1941 The second anti-Semitic Statute des Juifs [Jewish Statute] is enacted by the French Vichy government. It subjects French or foreign Jews to administrative internment for violation of the Statute des Juifs or for any reason whatsoever. The law removes the boundaries between French and foreign Jews. A person could even be interned if "suspected of being Jewish." Further laws calling for the expropriation and Aryanization of Jewish property are enacted. A mandatory inventory of Jewish property is demanded. Eventually, 42,000 Jewish businesses, buildings, homes, and other properties are confiscated.

June 3, 1941 U.S. State Department institutes policies discouraging and interfering with refugees from German-occupied territories.

June 11, 1941 Eichmann announces plans to deport 100,000 Jews from France in the coming three months. The plan is to deport 22,000 Jews from Paris and 10,000 from Vichy.

June 22, 1941 German army invades Soviet Union; Nazi *Einsatzgruppen* (mobile killing squads) begin mass murder of Jews, civilians, and Communist leaders.

July 31, 1941 Heydrich appointed by Göring to implement the "Final Solution."
✚ 3,429 Jews are arrested and interned in the southern occupied zone. ✚ The Nazis order the closing of the emigration departments of the *Reichsvereinigung*

in Austria and Germany. Nazis ban emigration for Jews between 18 and 45 years old. The age is soon extended to 60 years old. ✚ A HICEM Report of August-September 1941 [The Hebrew Immigration Aid Society] CDJC, CDXIV-39, recorded that 30 or 40 American entry visas were issued daily [from the U.S. Consulate in Marseilles].

August 8, 1941 Deportation of 11,485 Jews begins from the Gurs and Rivesaltes camps in the southern zone.

October 1, 1941 All legal emigration out of German-occupied territories is stopped by Gestapo order. It is estimated that 163,000 Jews are still living in the Greater Reich.

October 4, 1941 The Conseil National de l'Eglise Réformée (National Council of the Reform Church) protests the deportation of Jews. It states, "Divine law does not allow families created at God's wish to be broken up, children separated from their mothers, the right of asylum and divine pity to be brushed aside, the respect for the human person to be violated and defenseless creatures to be delivered up to a tragic fate."

October 23, 1941 Himmler orders that no more Jews are to emigrate from the German-occupied zones. This order takes effect in France in February 1942.

Late October 1941 After being forced to leave Marseilles, Varian Fry returns to New York City. Fry eventually becomes *persona non grata* with the administrators of the ERC over Fry's policies in Marseilles.

November 1941 There are approximately 17,500 internees in French camps in the southern unoccupied zone. 11,150 are Jews (63%).

November 29, 1941 Under German pressure, Vichy orders the dissolution of all Jewish organizations. Their records must be turned over to Vichy officials. Vichy forms the Union General de Israelites du France (UGIF), which the Germans hope to turn into a *Judenrat* (Jewish Council). The UGIF refuses to take part in selecting Jews for deportation during the roundups. The UGIF helps Jews escape and provides them with food and shelter.

December 1941 The Swiss Red Cross launches a relief operation specifically to save French Jewish children. The Swiss Red Cross has delegations located in Paris, Marseilles, Lille, Lyons, Toulouse, and Arles.

December 7, 1941 Japanese attack Pearl Harbor. America declares war on Japan and, the next day, on Germany. . . . ✚ Night and Fog Decree: Hitler orders the suppression of anti-Nazi resistance in occupied Western Europe.

December 8, 1941 Gassing of Jews begins at Chelmno extermination camp in Poland.

December 14, 1941 Major deportations in France are announced. Due to lack of rail transportation, the deportations to the death camps do not begin until March 1942.

1942–1945 Varian Fry writes *Surrender on Demand*. It is his account of the rescue efforts of the Emergency Rescue Committee in southern France. He outlines in detail the activities of Hiram Bingham, Vladimir Vochoc, Gilberto Bosques, and other diplomats who helped Jews in southern France. It is published in 1945.

June 1942 In Marseilles, the Emergency Rescue Committee is forced to close by the French police for subversive activities in helping refugees. The ERC continues to operate secretly. The Villa Air-Bel estate outside Paris becomes a haven for the Alsatian refugees.

June 11, 1942 Himmler orders increased deportations to Auschwitz from southeastern Europe. He includes 100,000 Jews to be deported from both zones in France. The French are asked to revoke the citizenship of the deportees and even pay for the cost of their deportation, which is set at 700 DM per Jew.

June 26, 1942 French Interior Minister Pucheu orders internment for all Jews who are stateless or are no longer protected by the country of their origin.

June 27, 1942 Vichy is asked to round up 50,000 Jews from the southern zone for deportation. ✝ In Bordeaux, the SS sends a train to deport the Jews there. In a lightening raid, the SS could find only 150 stateless Jews. Eichmann is furious and cancels the train transport. Eichmann says, "This never happened before."

June 30, 1942 Adolph Eichmann arrives in Paris with an order from Himmler to deport all Jews, regardless of whether they are French citizens or not.

July 16, 1942 In two days, 12,884 Jews are arrested in Paris and are interned in Drancy, pending deportation—4,051 are children.

July 20, 1942 French Ministry of the Interior suspends issuing exit visas for foreign Jews except for those from the Benelux countries.

July 27, 1942 French officials order the roundup of between 3,000 and 4,000 Jews in the occupied zone. These deportations are to be carried out by French police. ✝ Germans demand that 32,000 Jews be deported by the end of the summer of 1942.

July 1942 Deportation of Jews from France to killing centers in Poland. 42,000 Jews are sent to their deaths, at least one-third of them from the unoccupied zone. ✝ The roundup of Jews is supported by Vichy officials and accomplished by the French police. Other than Bulgaria, this was the only case in which a sovereign country in Western Europe signed a contract for the deportation of its Jews. ✝ Deportation of Jewish refugees is defied, and Jews are hidden in secret rescue and relief organizations. These organizations, both Jewish and non-Jewish, hide Jews, move them to safe havens, provide them with food, forged documents and passports. Jews are also helped to escape from French concentration camps. ✝ In Paris, French officials warn Jews of impending arrests, and they are able to escape. ✝ In the southern zone of Lyons, General Robert de Saint-Vincent refuses to use his military troops in the roundup and deportation of Jews. He is immediately relieved of his command. Other French officials refuse to participate in the deportations and resign their commissions rather than participate.

August 26-28, 1942 7,100 Jews are deported from the unoccupied zone. This is way below the German demand.

August 1942 25,000 Jews in France are deported to Auschwitz. Most of them are murdered upon arrival. ✝ Following the mass deportations of Jews from the occupied and unoccupied zones of France, Spain's border continues to be a vital escape route for Jewish refugees. By October, several hundred Jewish refugees have escaped across the border.

September 1942 27,000 Jews in 13 separate deportations are sent to Auschwitz from both French zones. These deportations are accomplished with the cooperation of French authorities and police. ✙ A network throughout the southern zone is established by Amitié Chrétienne [Christian Friendship]. Refugees are hidden in convents and churches. Escape routes are established from Toulouse to Spain and from Lyons, Grenoble, and Valence to Switzerland. Clergy in Haute-Savoie become guides. The nuns of Notre-Dame-de-Sion in Lyons provide forged documents. Protestant hostels in Lyons are used as refuges. ✙ Monsignor Rémond, Bishop of Nice, forbids the checking of baptismal certificates by anti-Jewish police. On September 30, a report states, "it is of public notoriety that he [the bishop] sets himself up as champion in defense of the Jews." ✙ Metro-Goldwyn-Mayer corporation donates one million dollars toward rescue of Jews in southern France.

November 1942 U.S. breaks off diplomatic relations with Vichy France. ✙ Some French police continue to sabotage deportations.

November 9, 1942 The Law of 1942 forbids foreign Jews in France from leaving. Vichy closes all of its borders and cancels all exit visas. Vichy ceases issuing visas to Jews.

December 10, 1942 Hitler orders all Jews to be deported from France to the German-occupied territories of the east. This includes enemies of the state, Communists, and Gaullists. This order is not conveyed to French officials. ✙ In preparation for the deportations, all Jews are evacuated from coastal or border departments. All Jews, with the exception of British, American, or other neutrals, are ordered to be arrested. In most cases, only three days' notice is provided to the Jews.

December 17, 1942 The United States, Great Britain, Belgium, Czechoslovakia, Poland, Yugoslavia, and the French government in exile make a joint declaration of condemnation against the murder of European Jews. They declare their intention to prosecute Nazi war criminals after the war. This declaration makes headlines around the world. Thousands of letters are sent to the U.S. State Department and the British Foreign Ministry at Whitehall regarding this declaration.

January 22-27, 1943 Ten thousand French police and several thousand German soldiers are sent to move the 22,000 residents of the old port of Marseilles and destroy it. In the process, 2,000 Jews are arrested.

February 1943 There may be as many as 140,000 Jews in the south of France, not including the Italian zone.

February 18, 1943 French police are ordered to round up French and foreign Jews and send them to the Gurs concentration camp, and then to Drancy. The Germans have limited success in this action due to increasing French resistance.

March 1943 The U.S. State Department blocks the rescue of 70,000 Jews from France and Romania by refusing to transfer money to support a plan worked out by Gerhardt Riegner of the World Jewish Congress. Funds are blocked in Swiss bank accounts until the end of the war. Agents of the Treasury Department discover this intentional delaying of the transfer of money. They determine that this is being done by Breckinridge Long and other officials at the State Department. A report on these activities is eventually submitted to Henry Morgenthau, Secretary of the Treasury. Morgenthau submits this report to President Roosevelt, which eventually leads to the creation of the War Refugee Board.

1996 Varian Fry is honored by the title of Righteous Among the Nations by the State of Israel. A tree is planted in Yad Vashem by U.S. Secretary of State Warren Christopher, along with Fry's son. Christopher apologizes for the State Department's treatment of Fry. Harry Bingham is honored in the "Visas for Life" exhibit for his work in helping Jewish refugees in Marseilles in 1940–1941. He is nominated for the title Righteous Among the Nations by the "Visas for Life" project.

June 27, 2002 American Foreign Service Association posthumously awards Hiram Bingham with the Constructive Dissent award. His citation reads: "His actions violated the State Department anti-refugee policy… [and showed] his willingness to put humanity before his career. . . ." The award was presented by Secretary of State Colin Powell.

December 2004 "Visas for Life" project nominates members of the Emergency Rescue Committee (ERC) for title Righteous Among the Nations.

2005 United States Postal Service announces it will issue a commemorative postage stamp in honor of Hiram "Harry" Bingham. ✤ Harry Bingham receives Letter of Recognition from Yad Vashem for his activities in Marseilles on behalf of Jews.

May 30, 2006 United States Postal Service issues commemorative stamp with the image of Hiram Bingham IV, as part of a set of six stamps titled "Distinguished American Diplomats."

The above historic timeline, mainly of events that occurred in France during World War II, was extrapolated from a timeline kindly supplied by Eric Saul, Director, Visas for Life Program, Simon Wiesenthal Center, Los Angeles, California.

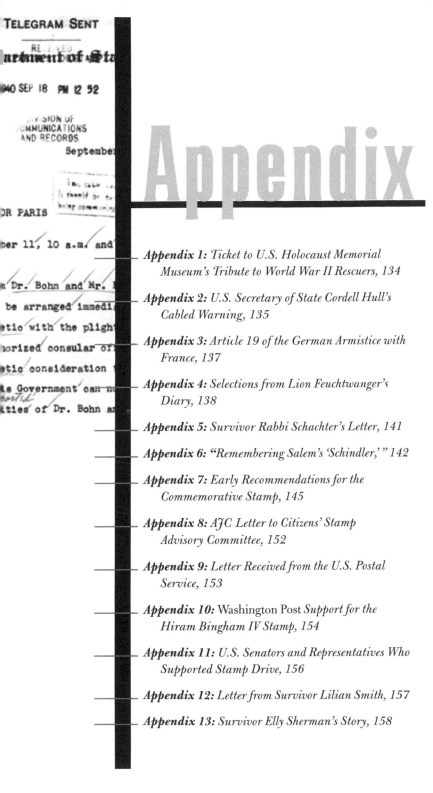

Appendix 1

Rose and Harry Bingham's ticket to the U.S. Holocaust Memorial Museum's 1993 Tribute to World War II Rescuers at Arlington National Cemetery. (Harry Bingham had already died in 1988, unknown to the Holocaust Museum.) This invitation was the first inkling to Harry Bingham's family that he was recognized as a "rescuer" by any group or organization.

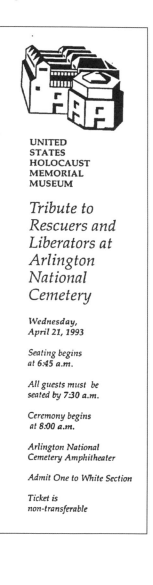

UNITED
STATES
HOLOCAUST
MEMORIAL
MUSEUM

*Tribute to
Rescuers and
Liberators at
Arlington
National
Cemetery*

*Wednesday,
April 21, 1993*

*Seating begins
at 6:45 a.m.*

*All guests must be
seated by 7:30 a.m.*

*Ceremony begins
at 8:00 a.m.*

*Arlington National
Cemetery Amphitheater*

Admit One to White Section

*Ticket is
non-transferable*

Appendix 2

U.S. Secretary of State Cordell Hull's cabled warning to Varian Fry and Dr. Bohn of the Emergency Rescue Committee—"and other persons."

In this two-page telegram, sent September 18, 1940, to the American Embassy, Vichy, Secretary of State Hull condemned "the activities of Dr. Bohn and Varian Fry and other persons, however well-meaning their motives may be." Just at that time, Harry Bingham was conducting underground rescue efforts in Marseilles with Bohn and Fry, giving out visas to "unfortunate refugees" to escape the Nazis.

Harry Bingham was subsequently transferred to Buenos Aires where he was passed over for promotions and resigned from the Foreign Service in 1945.

PREPARING OFFICE
WILL INDICATE WHETHER

TELEGRAM SENT

TO BE TRANSMITTED
CONFIDENTIAL CODE
NONCONFIDENTIAL CODE
PARTAIR
PLAIN

Collect
Full rate
Day letter
Night letter

Charge Department:
Full rate
Day letter
Night letter

Charge to
$

Department of State

Washington,

-2-

consular offices as meeting the requirements of American
immigration laws have the required visa documentation to
proceed to the United States, this Government does not
repeat not countenance any activity by American citizens
or other persons desiring to evade the laws of the governments with which this country maintains friendly relations.
You may also ask Mr. Hurley to inform the Prefect at
Marseille in this sense. Consul at Marseille should
also be informed that Dr. Bohn has been requested to
return to United States immediately. You may also advise
Embassy Paris and Consuls at Bordeaux and Nice regarding
situation. Keep Department advised of developments.

811.111 Refugees/267

VD:EBC:MLS

Enciphered by ....

Sent by operator .... *M.,* .... *19.* ....

Appendix 3

Article 19 of the German Armistice with France in 1940, as cabled from Berlin by the Associated Press, is quoted in full in Fry's original manuscript for Surrender on Demand. *(His published book gives a shorter version of Article 19.)*

The manuscript, never published, is in the possession of the Rare Book and Manuscript Section of Columbia University.

All German war and civil prisoners in French custody, including those under arrest and convicted who were seized and sentenced because of acts against the German Reich, shall be surrendered immediately to German troops. The French Government is obliged to surrender upon demand, all Germans named by the German Government in France, as well as in French possessions, Colonies, Protectorate, Territories and Mandates. The French Government binds itself to prevent removal of German war and civil prisoners from France into French possessions or into foreign countries. Regarding prisoners already taken outside of France, as well as sick and wounded German prisoners who cannot be transported, exact lists with the places of residence are to be produced. The German High Command assumes care of sick and wounded German war prisoners.

Appendix 4

Selections from Lion Feuchtwanger's 1940 diary.
Original German version courtesy of Feuchtwanger Memorial Library,
Specialized Libraries and Archival Collections, University of Southern California.
Translation is by William Endicott.

Sunday 21, July

Very bad night. Stomach pains. Beautiful day. Headache. Made an excursion with the Wolf brother and their nephews. Went very lazily through a German-appearing landscape. Pretty river with a big monastery on it. Ate very well in a rural restaurant. Golo Mann and Rheinhart joined us. Slept afterwards. Bothered by light cold and headache. Then, on the way home, Madame Lekisch appears at the place where you go down to the swimming hole and explains that I must go to Marseille. She shows a letter from Marta, it's a serious matter. At the same time, an American clothed in white, Consul Standish, is there with an elegant diplomatic auto. I have to get in. He explains to me that he will probably have the possibility of carrying me away in a Red Cross ship. He dresses me up a bit in a blanket and a shawl and dark sunglasses. He does not allow me to get my bag even though we drive close by the camp. I . . . tell them to send my bag to Sanary. Then, fearful of every Gendarme, to Nimes, but everything goes well. He takes care of the Gendarmes very carefully. In a small restaurant, we meet his wife and a friend of his. My frightful headache gets better after an aspirin. Then we drive quickly to Marseille, with me still dressed up. We are checked once again by the police, but everything goes all right. Suddenly I arrive at another Consul, Bingham's. On the way I learn that the State Department has sent a telegram saying that every consideration should be given me. But it is difficult with the two Consuls, the two young men being so well-intentioned. The English conversation in the fast moving auto is very difficult for me. Also, I am bothered by stomach ache, headache and general weakness. Then in Bingham's house, Marta greets me. Very quickly it appears that the story with the Red Cross will in no way be simple. The good-natured, embarrassed Bingham gradually explains to me several details about the escape plan that do not sound very promising. Went to dinner. The toilet facilities in the house are not simple.

Marseille, Monday, 22 July

Bingham is an awkward, friendly, puritanical, dutiful, somewhat sad New Englander, who is very attached to his wife. He very much misses her and his children who have been removed to America. The servants are bad and not very friendly. Bingham tells about all the work that emigrants are making for him. He is always tired and exhausted. . . .

Marseille, Sunday, 28 July

With Bingham personal understanding is getting better. Towards evening, however, while I am speaking with him, he gets a telephone call from his consul-general, which puts him into a sharp conversation. It's about a quite unimportant matter, but he is totally troubled, and I fear that my own thing will be unfavorably influenced by this coincidence. Nevertheless, he explains very confidentially about his difficult position in the Consulate, and our personal relations improve.

Marseille, Monday, 29 July

At noon Lilo arrives. In the camp on the day of my abduction French officers, who were supposed to bring me away, were looking for me. When they can't find me, there is great excitement and poor Wolf is suspected of an abduction in collaboration with the Nazis. Everything a bit dark. Lilo's husband is in Sanary [French town where Feuchtwanger had been living for eight years]. In our house a certain Joachim, a refugee is also lodging. In the evening Bingham is in a happier mood. For the moment, his clash with the consul-general has had no consequences. General conversation about national economic problems.

Sunday, 4 August

Bingham hints that I should leave, he fears that it will be too dangerous for him if I stay too long in his house. After that he made a portrait of me. I read. Worked. Bingham expresses regret and explains that of course he still wants to keep me here.

Monday, 5 August

Just after she [Marta—his wife] left, my tent friend Wolf [a fellow transit camp internee] telephones. That's very pleasant. It's also good that the maid believes that the caller is Golo Mann and not Wolf, because Bingham is not supposed to know that with the exception of Golo Mann, no one knows that I am living in his house.

Wednesday, 7 August

Slept very badly. Wonderful weather. Standish and his wife are there for breakfast, I am awkward. Then, quite unexpectedly, Lilo arrives with her husband. . . .She says it is too dangerous for me to return to Sanary and advises that I should dog Bingham as long as possible and that I should try hard to obtain a fake French document. But Mr. Brousse, through whose intervention that might work, is not here. In the afternoon, spoke to kind Loewenbein, but he also had no advice. In the evening Standish is here again; he wants to speak with a flyer about whether he would perhaps fly me to Portugal.

Saturday, 10 August

At noon come Bingham and Standish. The latter explains that it won't work with the fake papers, they cost 50,000 francs. . . .

Appendix 4 (continued)

Sunday, 11 August

At noon Bingham brings the man from the American Federation of Labor [Frank Bohn?]. He explains that with regular procedures there is absolutely nothing that can be done. But he wants to put a smuggling boat at my disposal. Everything very adventurous but not quite hopeless.

Marseille, Monday, 12 August

Wonderful weather. Slept OK. The prospect of escape lifts my mood, but the impending hardships and dangers make me nervous. Worry about whether I can take Marta with me. But Bingham takes it as obvious. Worked a bit.

Saturday, 17 August

I try to suggest to Bingham that he should give me a visa with the name Wetcheek. He goes along with it and is happy that he thought of it himself. We have a lively conversation.

Then Bohn phones, and shares that the boat will indeed go, wants gas from the Wolfs. Bohn and another American from his people, Fry, eat here in the evening. Many problems emerge. Gabbed quite a lot with Bingham.

Thursday, 29 August

Bingham in a bad mood. I did not sleep long enough. A lot of unpleasant little things to think about. Then Wolf arrives and reports that the whole story with the exit visa and Toulouse has gone out the window and that they will probably be keeping careful watch on Mr. Wetcheek and Mrs. Feuchtwanger.

Big panic. Back and forth, what should one do if someone comes to Bingham enquiring about Wetcheek and so forth. A half hour later he calls, everything is over. It turns out that it certainly is not so simple but rather that the people with our passes have been arrested and now a big bribe must be paid to the police. Then Heinrich Mann arrives and reports in a depressed manner that the story about the boat has come to naught again. Then I'm supposed to meet an influential communist, but instead of that Kantorowicz stands in for him. Very tired. Evening with Bingham and Fry who comes late. I let the meal pass by without inquiring what exactly is wrong. Then I ask, and it turns out that the boat is not going and never will go. Instead of this, Fry suggests that we should under his protection simply go over the Spanish border illegally. The plan immediately takes shape and I quickly agree without delay. A lot of individual technical difficulties, but I am in a good mood because finally there is a tangible plan.

Appendix 5

Survivor Rabbi Schachter's letter.

In April 2003, survivor Rabbi Joseph Schachter sent the author the following e-mail. He learned about the Hiram Bingham IV stamp drive through the Internet. He and his family of six were saved by Harry Bingham in 1940.

April 13, 2003

Dear Mr. Bingham,

A friend sent me a news story regarding your late father describing his life's work and the delayed posthumous recognition. The story was accompanied with a request to pass it on to others which I was happy to do, with one important addition; to wit, the fact that I and my entire immediate family (six persons in all) had received the life-saving visas dated Feb. 7, 1941. Regulations required him to sign four times for each of us.

My sister, who has the originals, hastened to let all those to whom I had forwarded the news story know that it was more than just a supposition that he had issued the visas—but that she had the original documents.

There is very little I can tell you about the process of issuance—I was just 10 years old at the time and do not remember any details other than a sense of relief that we were going to be able to escape the impending disaster having already had three "brushes" with the Gestapo—in Vienna in 1938 from which we fled to Belgium, and from Antwerp which we fled in May 1940, and in the Occupied portion of France from which we managed to make our way south.

A little about our family:

Our parents—Salomon and Gitta Schachter accompanied by four children aged 17, 10, 8, and 7 were able to embark on Feb. 17 by way of the Antilles and reach US territory, the Virgin Islands in March. Our parents are gone now, but there are quite a number of grandchildren and great-grandchildren scattered in many parts of the United States and Canada, and some of us now reside in Israel. We have, as a result of the news story, passed on the very aspect of their existence as having been dramatically affected by the actions of Hiram Bingham IV.

It may be of interest to you to learn that my brother and I are Rabbis who have served in various capacities, my sister has been a teacher, and the youngest one is gone now (as are my parents). Whatever good any of us has ever done for whomever should be partially accredited to your father. To paraphrase my mother's saying: "When he reaches Paradise he will find a multitude of greeters welcoming him and thanking him!"

If we can be of any help in the project for a commemorative stamp, I'd be delighted to enlist the entire family and friends.

Sincerely, Rabbi Joseph Schachter

Appendix 6

"Remembering Salem's 'Schindler,'" by Robert Kim Bingham, reprinted from the Groton School Quarterly, *describing a tour of Israel by three of Harry Bingham's sons, who had been invited by the Simon Wiesenthal Center in Los Angeles. The article was originally printed in* The Day, *New London, Connecticut, May 24, 1998.*

"Remembering Salem's 'Schindler' "
By Robert Kim Bingham '60, P '85

On April 20, three sons of Salem's Hiram Bingham (who died in 1988) flew to Israel at the invitation of the Simon Wiesenthal Center in Los Angeles, for a 14-day tour of that country. The sons—David, Robert Kim, and William—and six other diplomatic families were welcomed by VIPs in Jerusalem, Galilee, and Tel Aviv.

Why were these families so recognized? A large municipal sign posted at Jerusalem's city limits said it all: "Israel Welcomes the Families of Diplomats Who Saved Jews from the Holocaust." They are the children, granddaughter and widow of the eleven "righteous diplomats" of eleven countries, officially honored by an exhibit opening on April 26 at Israel's Yad Vashem National Holocaust Museum, for their heroism in saving many lives from the Holocaust. Hiram Bingham is the only U. S. diplomat so acknowledged. While stationed in Marseilles as a vice consul from 1938 to 1941, my father saved about 2,500 Jewish artists, painters and others seeking to escape Europe through Vichy France.

Collectively, the eleven diplomats, at great personal risk to themselves, clandestinely saved 200,000 lives from the Holocaust, by writing visas and affidavits of eligibility for passage, and planning escapes from Europe, circumventing their superiors' orders. There are an estimated 1 million descendants of these survivors.

Hiram Bingham also hid refugees at his diplomatic villa, helping some of the most notable intellectuals and artists to escape, including Marc Chagall (painter), Lion Feuchtwanger (author), Golo Mann (historian and son of Thomas Mann), and Dr. and Mrs. Otto Meyerhof (Nobel Prize winning physicist) and their son Walter. . . .

My brothers and I attended the official opening of the exhibit and a ceremony at the Yad Vashem for the first day issue of Israel's new postage stamp recognizing several of the heroic diplomats. Because my father saved Marc Chagall, we were given a special tour of Marc Chagall's glass windows in the hospital temple in Jerusalem, which beautifully portray the Twelve Tribes of Israel.

The trip was very emotional. Many survivors of the Holocaust gave speeches of gratitude and personal accounts of their own families' escapes from Europe during

World War II. At a place called the "Bible Park," between Jerusalem and Tel Aviv, the Bingham sons hugged the granddaughter of a survivor who had escaped Europe through Marseilles, when our father was there. She happened to be the official guide for Bible Park and we now have her photograph. Other families met survivors saved by their diplomatic fathers.

Our visit to the Yeshiva orthodox law center in Jerusalem was also very moving. Three survivors saved by Chiune Sugihara, the Japanese consul in Lithuania, expressed profound gratitude to Mrs. Sugihara, his widow. One spoke of his escape from the Holocaust. When he was only six years old, a neighbor boy led him away up the street (by prearrangement of the parents). He looked back for his mother, who was standing at the second floor window of their house, looking down at him while he was proceeding to Sugihara's visa office. As he spotted her, she closed her eyes and kept her mouth shut. She could not wave to him. He cried, "Mommy, Mommy," but she did not respond—and he never saw her again. Everyone in the crowded Rabbi's conference room was in tears, including the speaker, who then embraced the frail Mrs. Sugihara, whose husband had given him the visa in Lithuania.

My father's devotion to good works came, in part, from our family's missionary zeal. Hiram I and II were Hawaiian missionary leaders in the last century. Hiram III was a governor and U.S. senator from Connecticut. Instead of saving souls and entering politics, Hiram IV, who seemed to walk in the shadow of his more famous father, was a humble, deeply religious Episcopalian, who saved many lives from the Holocaust. My mother Rose was also a "woman of valor." She was a devoted wife and mother who was sent back to the United States from Marseilles with four children, while German U2 boats patrolled the Atlantic, so that Hiram could carry on his activities in Marseilles. They were separated for eighteen months. When he returned to the States briefly before his next assignment to Buenos Aires, Argentina (where I was born), my father appeared frail to her, had white hair and was a chain smoker. My mother hardly recognized him, but their underlying devotion to each other caused them to renew their wedding vows and to begin life anew.

At a dinner in Jerusalem's Renaissance Hotel, a group of Orthodox Jews who had heard of the diplomatic families' presence came by our table. Our guide introduced them to us. Two were survivors who had been saved by Oscar Schindler, whom they knew well. Two others had been saved by Raoul Wallenberg. One of the latter gratefully remarked, "You righteous gentiles honor us wherever you sit." One man said that he was unimpressed with official titles such as "president" or "chairman of this or that." What counted most to him was that our fathers were the rescuers, he said, and thanked us for coming.

On April 26, my brothers and I planted a tree for Hiram in the Sugihara Forest on a beautiful hillside overlooking Jerusalem. The tree is the fourth in a semicircle of pines officially planted in honor of the eleven righteous diplomats.

Appendix 6 (continued)

While growing up, I never knew the extent of my father's exploits. He never told me a great deal about his experiences during World War II. A number of other diplomatic family members likewise indicated that they had only recently made such discoveries.

Throughout my stay in Israel, I was reminded of the old song, "Oh, My Papa, to Me You Were So Wonderful," which has always been close to the surface of my thoughts. I recall tearfully singing it to my father ten years ago as he lay handsomely in his coffin awaiting burial in the family cemetery.

May his goodness and values live in the tree planted in his honor, over the city of Jerusalem, forever.

Appendix 7

Early recommendations for the commemorative stamp, honoring Hiram Bingham IV, sent to U.S. Postmaster General William Henderson, December 1998 and December 1999.

December 30, 1998

Honorable William J. Henderson
Postmaster General
United States Postal Service
475 L'Enfant Plaza, SW
Washington, DC 20260-1540

Recommendation:

Issue Commemorative Stamp Featuring Hiram Bingham IV, World War II "Righteous Diplomat" Who Saved Thousands of Refugees From Holocaust

Dear Mr. Postmaster:

I respectfully recommend that the United States Postal Service issue a commemorative stamp in honor of my father Hiram Bingham IV, a World War II diplomatic hero (who died in January 1988), for the following reasons:

Basis for recommendation:

1. Hiram Bingham IV saved between 2500 and 5000 refugees as they fled Hitler's occupied Europe through Marseilles. At great personal danger, he conducted clandestine rescue efforts with Varian Fry and others, against his superiors' policies, and harbored many refugees at his diplomatic residence in Marseilles, France, where he was stationed as U.S. Consul from 1939–1941.

2. Hiram Bingham IV helped some of the most notable intellectuals and artists escape, including Marc Chagall, painter; Lion Feuchtwanger, author; Golo Mann, historian, son of Thomas Mann; and Dr. and Mrs. Otto Meyerhof, Nobel Prize winning physicist, and their son Walter. . . .

3. America, Connecticut and the Town of Salem (Connecticut) can be proud of their native son, Salem's "Schindler," whose story is now unfolding, fifty years later. . . . The eleven "righteous diplomats" are:

Hiram ("Harry") Bingham of the United States, in Marseilles, France

Aristides De Sousa Mendes, of Portugal, in Bordeaux, France

George Dickuitz of Germany, in Copenhagen, Denmark

Feng Shan Ho of China, in Vienna, Austria

Paul Komor of Hungary, in Shanghai, China

Carl Lutz of Switzerland, in Budapest, Hungary

Giorgio Perlasca' an Italian possessing temporary Spanish citizenship, in
Budapest, Hungary

Chiune Sugihara of Japan, in Kovno, Lithuania

Raoul Wallenberg and Per Anger of Sweden, in Budapest, Hungary

Jan Zwartendijk of Holland, in Kaunas, Lithuania

Collectively, these eleven men, at great personal risk to themselves, clandestinely saved 200,000 lives from the Holocaust, by writing visas and affidavits of eligibility for passage, and planning escapes from Europe, in derogation of their superiors' orders. Today, there are an estimated one million descendants of these survivors, yet "many people in the world have still not learned of these great men and their families," according to the Simon Wiesenthal Center.

The curator of the Simon Wiesenthal Center continues to gather all pertinent information and is discussing the possibility of having an exhibit of the righteous diplomats at the United Nations, at the Capitol in Washington, DC, and in Paris, France; Bern, Switzerland; and the European Parliament, in Strasbourg.

4. Hiram Bingham IV is uniquely qualified for the honor of a commemorative postage stamp since his heroism involves federal service that has received bipartisan praise.

5. On February 11, 1998, Senator Joe Lieberman of Connecticut recounted the "Bingham story" on the Senate floor, speaking in support of Hiram's nomination by the Yad Vashem as a "Righteous Gentile." (See Senator Lieberman's tribute to Hiram Bingham IV in the Congressional Record.) In April 1998, Connecticut Lieutenant Governor Jodi Rell gave a stirring tribute to Hiram Bingham IV during Holocaust ceremonies at the State House, as a heroic, compassionate, son of Connecticut.

6. Hiram Bingham IV's WWII activities have already been featured at museums: On April 24, 1998, an exhibit opened at the Yad Vashem, Israel's National Holocaust Museum, featuring the eleven righteous diplomats, including Hiram Bingham. "Hiram's wall" contained his large photograph and documents relating to his exploits in Marseilles. He has also been featured in exhibits at the Simon Wiesenthal Center in Los Angeles and at the Jewish Heritage Museum in New York City, and in memorabilia at the Holocaust Memorial Museum in Washington, DC.

7. Hiram Bingham IV, the only United States Diplomat who has been officially honored by the State of Israel as a "righteous diplomat" is increasingly so recognized by the American government, for his role in saving thousands of refugees from the Holocaust.

8. The State of Israel invited Harry's children and other foreign diplomatic

rescuers' families on a two-week VIP tour of Israel April 21–May 5, 1998. We were opening exhibit ceremonies at the Yad Vashem and to 50th anniversary national celebrations. Harry's sons and six other diplomatic families were welcomed as VIPs at various receptions and dedications in Jerusalem, Galilee, and Tel Aviv. The families met with the Foreign Ministry of Israel; dined at the Japanese Embassy in Tel Aviv; shared breakfast with the American Ambassador; met with other ambassadors to Israel; received front-row seating at the National Holocaust Memorial ceremony and a warm personal greeting from Vice President and Mrs. Gore, after the Vice President's speech in Jerusalem on Israel's 50th Anniversary. Because Harry saved Marc Chagall, the group was given a special tour of Marc Chagall's glass windows in the hospital temple in Jerusalem which beautifully portray the Twelve Tribes of Israel. The families also attended a ceremony for the first day issue of Israel's new postage stamp which featured several of these eleven heroic diplomats.

9. When touring Israel, we were greeted by a large municipal sign posted at Jerusalem's city limits declaring: "Israel Welcomes the Families of Diplomats Who Saved Jews From the Holocaust." Vice President Al Gore and Mrs. Gore greeted the families, after speaking in Jerusalem.

10. On April 26, the three Bingham sons planted a tree for Hiram at a nationally televised ceremony in the Sugihara Forest overlooking Jerusalem. Hiram's tree is the fourth in a semicircle of pines officially planted in honor of the eleven righteous diplomats. It was extremely moving leaving a memorial in Israel to Hiram's goodness.

Personal note: *Tour of Israel.* While growing up, I never knew the extent of my father's exploits until I read details published by the Simon Wiesenthal Center, saw the descriptive plaques on "Hiram's Wall" at the Yad Vashem National Holocaust Museum in Jerusalem, and greeted people in Israel. I had always known about Marc Chagall (whom my father admired tremendously), Lion Feuchtwanger, Varian Fry (civilian rescuer), and the other persons apparently on a list provided to Harry by Mrs. Eleanor Roosevelt. In later years, my father painted oil copies of Chagall's works, which have hung in the Salem Mumford House for decades. (This association added to the poignancy of experiencing Chagall's exquisite stained glass windows in Jerusalem.)

The "Visas for Life Tour" of Israel was very emotional for this writer. Many survivors of the Holocaust gave speeches of gratitude to these eleven diplomats and personal accounts of their own families' escapes from Europe during WWII. We responded by speaking about our fathers. At a place called the "Bible Park" between Jerusalem and Tel Aviv, the Bingham sons hugged the granddaughter of a survivor who had escaped Europe through Marseilles when our father was stationed there. She happened to be the official guide for the Bible Park, and we now have her photograph. Other families joyously met survivors saved by their diplomatic fathers.

Our visit to the Yeshiva orthodox law center in Jerusalem also was very moving. Three survivors saved by Mr. Sugihara, the Japanese consul in Lithuania, expressed profound gratitude to Mrs. Sugihara, his widow. One spoke of his escape from the Holocaust. When he was only six years old, a taller neighbor boy came and led him away up the street (by prearrangement of the parents). He looked back for his mother, who was standing at the second floor window of their house, looking down at him while he was proceeding to Sugihara's visa office. As he spotted her, she closed her eyes and kept her mouth shut. She could not wave to him. He cried "Mommy, Mommy!" but she did not respond—and he never saw her again. Everyone in the crowded Rabbi's conference room was in tears, including the speaker, who then embraced the frail Mrs. Sugihara whose husband had given him the visa that day in Lithuania.

My mother, Rose, also was a "woman of valor." She was a devoted wife and mother who was sent back to the United States from Marseilles with four children, while German U2 boats patrolled the Atlantic, so that Harry could carry on his activities in Marseilles. They were separated for 14 months. When he returned to the States briefly before his next assignment to Buenos Aires, Argentina (where this writer was born), my father appeared frail to her, and now had white hair. My mother hardly recognized him, but their underlying devotion to each other caused them to renew their marriage vows, to begin life anew (and eventually beget eleven children).

When we were growing up in Salem (from 1945 until his death in 1988), my father always reminded his eleven children of a personal motto he developed, which, paraphrased, was "Give the best that you have to the best that you know." When given the opportunity as a government officer, he delivered many from evil. He resigned from the Foreign Service not long after his heroic efforts during WWII, moving to Salem, Connecticut, in 1945 to raise his large family on an inherited farm.

During our "Visas for Life Tour of Israel," at one dinner in the Renaissance Hotel in Jerusalem, a group of Orthodox Jews who had heard of the diplomatic families' presence came and stood by our table. Our tour guide introduced them to us. Two of them were survivors who had been saved by Otto Schindler, whom they personally knew well. Two others had been saved by Raoul Wallenberg. One of the latter, a professor, gratefully remarked, "You righteous gentiles honor us wherever you sit." Two of the owners of the hotel were there, and one whom Schindler had saved said to his fellow attendees, "We should be very proud—because of them we are alive." When Schindler came to Israel, he visited the man's house and called the man's children, and all Jewish children, "my children." In expressing gratitude to the diplomatic families, the man said that he was unimpressed with official titles such as "President" or "Chairman of this or that." What counted most to him was that our fathers were the rescuers "and we thank you for being here."

My father, a humble man who did not boast of his activities, never told me a great deal about his experiences during WWII. A number of other diplomatic family members likewise indicated that they had only recently made such discoveries about their relatives (thanks, undoubtedly, to the initiatives of the respective museums, their curators, and researchers).

I was grateful to hear histories of several survivors during our tour of Israel, as their expressions of gratitude inspired feelings of deep pride for my father, who was being celebrated in the august group of heroic diplomats. The trip abounded in serendipitous encounters: for instance, the chance meeting on our second-to-last day with the guide of a preserve called Bible Park, who was the granddaughter of a woman who had escaped the Holocaust through Marseilles. This was a moving and emotional experience for my brothers and me.

I believe that my father's devotion to good works came, in part, from our family's long missionary zeal. Hirams I and II were Hawaiian missionary leaders in the last century, depicted in James Michener's novel *Hawaii*. Hiram III, apart from earning fame as the explorer who discovered Machu Picchu in Peru, was a politician and became a Connecticut Governor and U.S. Senator. Instead of converting souls or solving political issues, Hiram IV, who walked in the shadow of his more famous father, the explorer, was a humble, deeply religious, Episcopalian who saved many lives from the Holocaust.

Attached are documents submitted in support of the instant recommendation to issue a commemorative stamp. . . .

I would be happy and honored to discuss this matter further with you. I am a senior government attorney in the Office of the General Counsel, United States Department of Justice, Immigration and Naturalization Service, at Hartford, Connecticut.

Sincerely Yours,

Robert Kim Bingham

December 18, 1999

Honorable William J. Henderson
Postmaster General
United States Postal Service
475 L'Enfant Plaza, SW
Washington, DC 20260-1540

Dear Mr. Henderson,

As coordinator of the stamp drive for Hiram Bingham IV, I am pleased to announce widespread support for the issuance of a commemorative stamp in the likeness of Hiram Bingham IV, WWII Holocaust Hero, "America's Wallenberg." I also wish to thank you for acknowledging the various letters and petitions of support submitted by distinguished citizens, lawmakers, organizations, and ordinary Americans, and I enclose copies of supporting documentation for inclusion in your Hiram Bingham IV stamp proposal file.

For your information, the Governor of Connecticut, John G. Rowland, has proclaimed April 3, 2000 as "Hiram Bingham IV Day" since that is the date of the opening of the United Nations "Visas for Life" exhibition honoring the several recognized WWII "righteous diplomats," including United States citizen Hiram Bingham IV, who together saved over 200,000 lives from the Holocaust. Elie Wiesel, distinguished survivor of the Holocaust, has accepted honorary chairmanship of this exhibition and will speak at the opening. National and international media attention will be generated for the exhibit and the small group of diplomats who saved over 200,000 Jews during the Holocaust, amounting to one million descendants of survivors today. The United Nations will send press releases to the various news agencies. I understand that a number of high officials will attend the opening of the exhibit, including Secretary of State Madeleine Albright, U.N. Secretary General Kofi Annan (who is married to Raoul Wallenberg's niece), the U.N. High Commissioner for Human Rights, surviving diplomats who rescued Jews, and current members of the diplomatic corps and General Assembly of the United Nations.

The local press has published headlines regarding the instant Hiram Bingham IV stamp drive and has referred to him as America's "Schindler." The story of Hiram Bingham IV also has captured the attention of the *New York Times*. See, for example, article by Maura Casey, *Connecticut Section*, Sunday, July 11, 1999. In addition, since he was an American diplomat, he is increasingly referred to as "America's Wallenberg."

Because the U.S. Postal Service issued a stamp for Swedish diplomat Raoul Wallenberg, I believe an equally compelling case is made for issuance of a U.S. postage stamp in the likeness of United States citizen Hiram Bingham IV, WWII diplomatic Holocaust hero who saved 2500–5000 lives. His courageous actions exemplified the finest service a public servant can give to his or her country. This is a heartwarming story all Americans can be proud of, that brings hope to those battling evil forces in the world, and can be kept alive by issuance of a commemorative stamp honoring Hiram Bingham IV.

I and Hiram's other sons, David and William, had the honor of attending the April 1998 opening of the Yad Vashem exhibit for the "righteous diplomats" in Jerusalem during Israel's 50th Anniversary. We toured Israel and witnessed the profound and moving respect given to such diplomats by the survivors of the Holocaust. My brothers and I also participated in a televised planting of a tree in memory of Hiram Bingham IV, which now stands in a semi-circle of pines representing the eleven righteous diplomats on a beautiful hillside overlooking Jerusalem. We also heard heartfelt stories of escapes from the Holocaust, including one told by a rabbi I will not forget. When he was six years old, an eight-year-old neighbor led him up the street to the visa office in Lithuania, by prearrangement of the parents. He looked back at his mother who watched with her head bowed from behind the second floor apartment window. He waved and cried, "Mommy, mommy!" but she did not wave back at him. He never saw her again. The rabbi finished the story with tears in his eyes. Then he embraced the elderly Mrs. Sugihara (standing there with us), who is the widow of the Japanese diplomat, Chiune Sugihara, who had issued him the forged visa that day over fifty years ago.

My own father's role in placing humanity above career poignantly came into focus during the tour of Israel. I remain hopeful that you and the United States Postal Service will elect to unveil a stamp in the likeness of the United States citizen Hiram Bingham IV, "Salem's Schindler," in an official ceremony here in his beloved rural hometown of Salem, Connecticut (where he died at age 85 in 1988), before the 100th Anniversary of his birth, July 17, 2003.

I thank you for considering this stamp proposal.

Sincerely,

Robert Kim Bingham, Esq., son of Hiram Bingham IV

Appendix 8

American Jewish Committee (AJC) letter sent to Citizens' Stamp Advisory Committee, December 1999.

The American Jewish Committee
The Jacob Blaustein Building
155 E. 56th St.
New York, NY 10622

December 7, 1999

Dr. Virginia Noelke, Chairperson
Citizens' Stamp Advisory Committee
475 L'Enfant Plaza , S.W.
Washington, D.C. 20260-2437

Dear Dr. Noelke:

We are writing to urge the Citizens' Stamp Advisory Committee to issue a commemorative stamp in honor of Hiram Bingham IV, an American hero of World War II. Mr. Bingham, who served as U.S. Consul in Marseilles, France, from 1939–1941, conducted clandestine rescue efforts and harbored many refugees at his diplomatic residence.

Hiram Bingham IV's activities saved between 2,000–5,000 people, mostly Jews, from the deadly grips of Nazi Germany. Among them were the renowned artist Marc Chagall; the distinguished author, Lion Feuchtwanger; noted historian Golo Mann; and Dr. Otto Meyerhof, a winner of the Nobel Prize in physics.

In recognition of his courage, Israel's Holocaust authority, Yad Vashem, has designated Mr. Bingham as one of 11 "Righteous Diplomats," and he is the only American among this group. His efforts are prominently displayed in the noted exhibition, "Visas for Life," which has traveled around the world and will open at the United Nations in early April 2000.

It is appropriate that our nation, too, honor this special hero, as it did several years ago when the United States Postal Service issued a commemorative stamp in honor of the legendary Swedish diplomat, Raoul Wallenberg. Hiram Bingham is America's Wallenberg, and as a Department of State employee, his heroic actions serve as an inspiration to all public servants, indeed to all Americans.

Appendix 9

Letter, dated May 11, 1999, received from the U.S. Postal Service.

May 11, 1999

Dear Mr. Bingham:

This is a follow up to your March 5 letter to Governor Fineman expressing support for the issuance of a commemorative stamp honoring Hiram Bingham IV. We regret the delay in responding to your inquiry.

You will be pleased to learn that the nomination of Hiram Bingham IV was reviewed by the Citizens' Stamp Advisory Committee at the April 22–23 meeting. The nomination was placed under consideration as a future stamp issuance. This Committee is responsible for reviewing stamp proposals and making subject and design recommendations to the Postmaster General.

There is no specific time frame for the issuance of stamp subjects. However, new stamps are announced approximately six months prior to the year in which the stamp will be issued. The Citizens' Stamp Advisory Committee works two to three years in advance to meet stamp design and production requirements. They are currently working on the stamp programs for 2002 and beyond.

Your interest in our stamp program is very much appreciated.

s/ Azeezaly S. Jaffer

Executive Director Stamp Services

Appendix 10

Support for the Hiram Bingham IV stamp from the Washington Post, *on July 28, 2001. The* Washington Post *published "Honor This Hero" by Ilene Munetz Pachman.*

"Honor This Hero"
By Ilene Munetz Pachman

Colin Powell began his tour as secretary of state with a stirring statement of respect for the professionalism and expertise of the Foreign Service, and a pledge to make full use of it during his time in office. In this spirit, I'd like to invite the secretary to join in an effort I've been working on for some time to honor another American diplomat, one who died 13 years ago without ever receiving his due from this country for the considerable services he rendered to humanity.

His name was Hiram "Harry" Bingham IV. The son of a U.S. senator from Connecticut (and former governor), he became an extraordinary unsung hero of the American diplomatic corps. Bingham jeopardized both his career and his life in the early years of World War II to help rescue between 2,500 and 5,000 Jews and anti-Nazi activists while he was stationed in Marseilles, France. For this work in the years 1939–41, he was reassigned (his wife was denied permission to join him) and held back professionally through the rest of his career.

Although Bingham in later years didn't talk much about his lifesaving work, he played a pivotal role in the rescue of many scholars and notable artists. Among them were a friend he greatly admired, painter Marc Chagall, and the anti-Nazi writer Franz Werfel, author of "The Song of Bernadette." As Robert Kim Bingham, one of his 11 children, noted, he put humanity before his career.

Hiram Bingham disregarded the orders of his superiors as he secretly issued visas and gave aid to thousands fleeing from the Nazis through southern France. Under the shadow of France's Vichy regime, he harbored many of the most wanted refugees at his diplomatic residence.

The summer of 1940 was a time when protecting Jews had become not only a dangerous act in France but, incredibly, a violation of U.S. State Department policies. Nonetheless, Bingham assisted U.S. journalist-turned-rescuer Varian Fry in implementing daring escapes. (Fry wrote that Bingham was his "partner in the 'crime' of saving human lives.")

Luminaries who were trapped in France and who in large measure owe their lives to Bingham include Nobel Prize-winning biochemist Otto Meyerhof; historical novelist Lion Feuchtwanger, known for his damning literary attack on Hitler; and historian Golo Mann, son of novelist Thomas Mann.

A decade after Bingham's death, his three sons had the honor of planting a tree for their father at Yad Vashem, in Jerusalem. He was among diplomats honored by Israel for breaking rules and laws to save lives during World War II.

Early in 1999, realizing the importance of an American symbol to memorialize his father, Kim Bingham wrote to the U.S. Postal Service's Citizens' Stamp Advisory Committee to propose the issuance of a commemorative stamp as a tribute. His quest for approval of a commemorative stamp is an uphill journey. Each year the CSAC receives proposals for some 2,000 different subjects. From these, the committee recommends a limited number to the postmaster general.

But the proposal for a Bingham stamp has gained the support of more than a third of the members of the U.S. Senate, and for good reason. Not only would it provide a belated honor to one who deserves it; such a stamp would serve as a reminder to the men and women of the Foreign Service that members of the diplomatic corps ought never lose sight of basic American principles—freedom, justice and human rights—in the conduct of the nation's foreign policy.

Ilene Munetz Pachman is a freelance writer.

Appendix 11

U.S. Senators and U.S. Representatives who supported the Hiram Bingham IV stamp drive. Also Connecticut legislature voted unanimously to support the stamp.

Here are the names of U.S. senators and U.S. representatives who supported the HBIV stamp proposal (see http://pages.cthome.net/WWIIHERO/).

U.S. Senators who signed a letter of support dated March 28, 2000, included: Joseph I. Lieberman, Christopher Dodd, Richard G. Lugar, Paul Wellstone, Wayne Allard, Max Cleland, Spencer Abraham, Charles E. Grassley, Thomas Daschle, Russell D. Feingold, Charles E. Schumer, Rod Grams, Patty Murray, Carl Levin, Chuck Hagel, Mike DeWine, John W. Warner, Richard H. Bryan, Fred Thompson, Robert Torricelli, Slade Gorton, Rick Santorum, Barbara Boxer, Paul S. Sarbanes, Richard J. Durbin, Arlen Specter, John Ashcroft, Frank R. Lautenberg, Daniel Patrick Moynihan, Robert J. Kerry, John F. Kerry, Barbara A. Mikulski, Edward M. Kennedy, Harry Reid, Gordon Smith, and Tim Johnson.

Thirty-five U.S. Representatives signed their support of the HBIV stamp proposal on March 9, 2000.

Sam Gejdenson, Norman Sisisky, Luis V. Gutierrez, Charles B. Rangel, Robert T. Matsui, Jerrold Nadler, Martin Frost, Howard L. Berman, Henry A. Waxman, Sander Levin, Bob Filner, Tom Lantos, Ileana Ros-Lehtinen, Michael R. McNulty, Bernie Sanders, Rush Holt, Grace F. Napolitano, John B. Larson, Dennis J. Kucinich, Steven C. LaTourette, Rosa L. DeLauro, Lloyd Doggett, Frank Pallone, Jr., Carrie P. Meek, Anthony Weiner, Pete Stark, Peter Deutch, Janice Schakowsky, Robert Wexler, Max Sandlin, Bob Borski, James Greenwood, John Lewis, David E. Bonior, Bob Etheridge. Subsequent endorsements by Rob Simmons and Chris Shays.

Regarding the amazing *unanimous* support of the Connecticut legislature on April 4, 2000. Congressman Simmons noted that "for the first time in history" all 151 state representatives and 36 senators endorsed a proposal without a dissent. When he served in the statehouse, he and Representative Linda Orange (D-Colchester) succeeded in gaining all state lawmakers' signatures.

A number of U.S. Senators from both sides of the aisle also submitted separate letters of support to the Citizens' Stamp Advisory Committee (CSAC). For example, Senator Joseph Lieberman wrote both the Chair of the CSAC and the Postmaster General in 2001; Senator Joseph R. Biden wrote to the CSAC in 2002; Senators Carl Levin, Arlen Specter, Max Cleland, and Rick Santorum wrote letters in 2002, and Frank Lautenberg wrote in 2003. Senator Joseph Lieberman also wrote Secretary of State Colin L. Powell in 2002, urging him to support the HBIV stamp proposal.

Appendix 12

Letter from survivor Lilian Smith, whose father was an anti-Nazi journalist wanted by the Gestapo. Harry Bingham rescued her, her brother, and her parents.

Dear Mr. Bingham,

Our son David, who went to Groton (but I believe graduated after you), has sent me the article which you contributed to the Groton Quarterly. I would like to add to your knowledge of your father's good deeds, which extended not only to Jewish artists and intellectuals such as those you mentioned, but also to non-Jewish people who were in trouble, such as my family.

In August of 1940, we were a French family in dire need to leave France: my father was a publisher of magazines and the owner of a press syndicate and had published and distributed a number of anti-Nazi articles, which had put him on the Gestapo list of people to be arrested.

He went to the American consul in Lyon to request visas for the U.S., where he had funds and his press syndicate had an office in New York (he had also represented an American press syndicate in Europe). Despite these assurances that we would not be a charge to the United States government, the consul in Lyon, going by the book, told my father that he could issue visas only to part of his family, suggesting that he leave two of his children behind to insure that we would come back! My father of course found this unacceptable and went on to Marseilles, where he had the great good luck to deal with your father.

We all came to the States. At the end of the war, my parents went back to France along with my younger sister. My brother and I became American citizens (my brother made his career in the U.S. Air Force after a stint in the Free French Air Force during the latter part of the war). I married an American who went into the Foreign Service. We have a son who went to Groton. During a parents' week end at Groton, we sat in the dining room next to a man who turned out to be your father. I cannot tell you how glad I was to use this remarkable coincidence to express my family's gratitude to him. He was a most generous and courageous man and there are now three generations of my family who should be grateful to your father. I thought you might like to know this.

Most sincerely,

Lilian Stuart Smith

Appendix 13

Survivor Elly Sherman's story.

Marseilles and How We Escaped Thanks to Hiram Bingham IV

The first time we were called to the police station and told to report in five days to Gurs, the French concentration camp in the Pyrenees mountains, Mother was ill and devastated. My sister Gerty and I decided to get advice from Uncle Otto. Well, he was not really our uncle but a man alone in Marseilles having come from Vienna after losing his wife and two daughters about our age. One never asked for details of such events knowing it was a most painful subject. It was a time when almost everyone had tragic events to deal with and one never asked "How" or "Why." Uncle Otto had taken Gerty and me under his wing and had given us permission to come to see him in his hotel if we were very very hungry and had nothing to eat and he would buy us a cup of watery chocolate and a breadstick at the cafe downstairs and this would often sustain us for the day.

When we told him that we had been called to report to the camp, his advice was straightforward: "You are both young and attractive" (my sister was 20 and I was 15). "Go to the chief of police, do what he wants and this way buy your way out." When we finally understood that we were to sit at the edge of the desk, raise our skirt over our knee and smile seductively we finally got the point and left. . . . But we were also assailed by doubts, we remembered the many stories of wives who, trying to obtain a husband's release from the Gestapo, tried the same route and when it was over were handed the husband in a jar containing his ashes. How could one possibly trust a Chief of Police to keep his word? By the time we returned to our hotel room, Mother had cabled her brother in New York and with the money he sent we bought our way out.

The second time we were called to report for internment, Mother was told by the Chief of Police that the Germans had become much more demanding, that the French had to turn over their quota of Jews, bribes would no longer work and the three of us had to report within two days. We were desperate. In the few days remaining we were frantically trying to get everything together for our escape. Mother again begged me to leave through the Quakers' program for children, as she had several times in the past year, but that would mean leaving without her or my sister and once again I refused: if I were saved and they did not make it I would hate what I would see in the mirror for the rest of my life. We would either all be saved, or none of us would be saved. And then with unbelievable luck all the necessary papers came through including the most difficult to obtain, the visa to the United States. The first thing in the morning was the walk to the U.S. Consulate to see whether our names were really on the list posted on the door. Then came the treks to try for all the other requirements: exit visa from France, transit visa from Martinique and of course, tickets for the next steamer. Since all of these had expiration dates, it was almost impossible to get "a full hand." It still seems a miracle that it happened for us.

It was not until many years later, in 2005, that I found out who had provided us with that precious visa. I received an e-mail of an article which mentioned the role Harry Bingham had played in France during the war years. The name seemed familiar, and I looked through the documents which had belonged to my now-deceased Mother. There it was: the original document granting the visa to my Mother, my sister and me, signed by Hiram Bingham, the red seal partly missing, the red ribbons a bit frayed but still there. . . .

It would be difficult to explain all the various feelings this has aroused, even now. I am so deeply grateful to this man who took such chances in helping us and so many others. All the events of that time come back in a rush, accompanied with many a tear, and a deep wish that my Mother and my Sister could be here to share in it. The past is ever with me, and although we were spared the worst, we were deeply aware of the fate of the ones who were not as lucky. Often I thought: "How do I know that this is not a dream, that I am really lying on the wooden cot in the camp, dreaming this dream that we are saved and in the United States." Often I also went through depression, feeling "Why me??" that "cri-de-coeur" as strong in this sense as in the sense of bemoaning one's miserable fate in life. Why was I saved? What must I do to merit this? How can I repay having received the gift of life?

But this gift, the gift of Hiram Bingham, and all my gratitude, is in the tears of my memories and in the laughter of my life.

Elly Sherman

Index